Women's Infidelity

LIVING IN LIMBO

What women really mean when they say, "I'm not happy."

Michelle Langley

McCarlan Publishing
P.O. Box 190424
St. Louis, Mo 63119

Library of Congress Control Number: 2005924375

ISBN 0-9767726-0-4

Copyright © 2005, Michelle Langley

All rights reserved. No part of this publication may be reproduced, stored in a retrieval system or transmitted in any form or by any means, electronic, mechanical, photocopy, recording or otherwise, without prior written permission from McCarlan Publishing, with the exception of short excerpts used with acknowledgment of publisher and author.

Excerpts from *The Alchemy of Lust* by Theresa L. Crenshaw, copyright © 1996, The Crenshaw Writing Company, Inc., used by permission of G. P. Putnam's Sons,
a division of Penguin Group (USA) Inc. Excerpts from *Divorced Dads* by Sanford L. Braver and Diane O'Connell, copyright © 1998, used by permission of Jeremy P. Tarcher, an imprint of Penguin Group (USA) Inc. Excerpts from *Craving for Ecstasy* by Harvey B. Milkman and Stanley G. Sunderwirth, copyright © 1987 by Jossey-Bass Inc. reprinted with permission of John Wiley & Sons, Inc. Permission granted by NBC to reprint transcripts from "Meet The Press," © 2005 NBC Universal, Inc., All Rights Reserved.

Editing and book design by Dianne Schilling
Cover design: Christine Thorwegen
Printed in the USA

*For Craig Langley,
with all of my love—then, now and always.*

*For my Mother,
whom I loved more than words can say.*

Acknowledgments

I owe a special debt of gratitude to my friend, Emily Boling, for being so helpful with this project. I appreciate all of the work she did and truly treasure her friendship. And I want to thank my friend, Carl Boyer, for helping me with the manuscript and for enriching my life in so many ways.

Heartfelt thanks to my friend, Stacey Brockus, for her never-ending support and encouragement. She has truly been an inspiration in my life. I would also like to express my sincere gratitude to my friend, Michele Brown, whom I appreciate more than words can say. This book would not have been possible without her. I am also grateful to her mother, Shirley Brown, who always makes me feel like part of the family.

Special thanks to Carolyn Carter for her help during the early stages of editing. She is a talented and gifted writer and I not only appreciate her help, I feel blessed to have her as a friend.

I want to thank Alan Clay for believing in me. I would never have typed a word had it not been for him. Thanks also to Harley Blosser for his much appreciated help and legal advice. And I want to acknowledge and thank Beth Mendes-Reynolds, whose extraordinary ability to lead and inspire I will always remember.

I would also like to thank Suzanne Fadin, Renay Jones, Ryan Nielson, Sherry Rhea, Nancy Tucker, Ryan Williams, and Tara Rose-Willis for their friendship and for all the joy they bring to my life.

A big thanks to my editor, Dianne Shilling. I found her honesty and directness in evaluating my work not only challenging, but inspiring. I can't say that without her there wouldn't have been a book, but I can say it probably wouldn't have been a very good one. Barbara was right, she is the best! Also, a special thanks to Christine Thorwegen for designing my cover. Her talent and creativity are greatly appreciated.

Particular thanks go to Daniel Padilla for helping to sharpen my memory during the final stages of the book. Special mention and thanks also go to Mike Smith.

Finally and most importantly I'd like to thank all of the women and men who shared their stories with me. This book would not have been possible without them.

Contents

Introduction ix

Chapter 1
Are Women Naturally Monogamous? 1
The stages of sexual desire women often experience after marriage

Chapter 2
The Sexual Devaluing System 21
Vaginal girls versus clitoral girls; The role of secrecy in female sexuality

Chapter 3
The Loss of Sexual Desire in Women 47
Is she really uninterested in sex, or is she just uninterested in sex with me?

Chapter 4
The Commitment Game: Female Version of Pursue and Discard .. 63
The female crisis; What do women really want sexually?

Chapter 5
The Allure of Affairs 81
Is it love or a crack high?

Chapter 6
Why Women Find Affair Sex Particularly Appealing 91
Does it take more than one man to please a woman sexually?
What is the cause of men's fear and denial?

Chapter 7
Women Aren't Just Angry, They Want Revenge 119
Do women today want men to pay for the sins of the past?

Chapter 8
Men Send Flowers, But Women Who Cheat Give Oral Sex 133
Tag: How women keep their husbands hanging on

Chapter 9
Women and Guilt 153
How women end up destroying their husbands emotionally because they don't want to hurt their feelings

Notes 183

About the Author 187

Introduction

Is infidelity women's best kept secret? Given that women initiate approximately 70 to 75 percent of all divorces, is this secret the catalyst that prompts them to pursue separations and divorces, many under the guise of "searching for self?" How many women who have had affairs were happily married prior to their affairs? Are men being divorced by their wives without ever knowing about their wives' extramarital relationships? Women's Infidelity discusses these and other wide-ranging, but interrelated, topics that help explain the difficulty women have with marriage and long-term fidelity.

Women's Infidelity also discusses society's continuing fear of women's sexuality as well as the myth that women are naturally monogamous and not inclined to desire multiple sexual partners. It is my opinion that women's lack of knowledge about their natural sexual impulses makes them much more likely than men to leave their marriages due to their sexual attractions and affairs.

Women's Infidelity will provide great insight and understanding to women who are secretly trying to choose between their husbands and their lovers, as well as men who are desperately trying to find the source of their wives' unhappiness.

I am not a physician or a psychologist. I began an independent inquiry into women's sexuality after my interest was sparked by a series of unrelated incidents. First, I discovered that two women I had known for years—both happily married—were having affairs. Then, a few weeks later, I had a particularly intriguing conversation with a complete stranger.

I had taken my car to a dealership for servicing. While I was sitting in an outdoor waiting area, a young female employee exited the building for a cigarette break. She appeared to be rather upset, so I asked her what was wrong. We ended up talking through her entire lunch hour. She said that she had been married for five years, but since the birth of her child had lost interest in having sex, so her husband wanted a divorce. She didn't seem to be bothered by disclosing such personal information so I asked her a question that under different circumstances might have been offensive.

"Does your disinterest in sex apply only to your husband?" I asked. She was surprised by my question, but began to describe her feelings. She explained that she was attracted to lots of men, even men she wouldn't normally find appealing. Sex with almost any man *except* her husband at times seemed desirable.

I began my research not long after that fateful conversation. I wanted to know if this woman's experiences—and my own—were normal. What the woman at the car dealership described sounded identical to what I was going through, except that I had no children.

Initially, I looked for answers in books. I also made several naive attempts to question female friends and family members. Their stonewalling fueled my interest further. I began to seek out and interview women wherever I went. Surprisingly, it wasn't difficult to get women to talk about their sexual desires and infidelities as long as no one else was present and they were assured anonymity. I interviewed some women only once; others I kept in contact with for years.

I interviewed men as well. Many were eager to talk about their marital difficulties. Eventually I was spending several hours a week in lengthy conversations with individuals, explaining the information I had gathered. By the time I stopped counting I had interviewed 123 women and 72 men.

The women and men I interviewed had varying socioeconomic backgrounds. The majority lived in the Midwest. However, 17 of those interviewed lived on either the east or west coast. Six of those interviewed were from different countries and only recently moved to the United States. Five were from the Middle East and one was from Africa.

The interviews were not always identical in regard to the questions asked. However, four questions were posed to every woman: Are you interested in having sex with your husband? Do you enjoy having sex with your husband? Do you think about or want to have sex with someone other than your husband? Have you had sex with someone other than your husband?

Several years into my research, I was able to identify distinctive patterns and behaviors in the women I interviewed. I categorized these into "stages" that women often experience during the course of their long-term relationships. The stages begin with a loss of sexual desire.

After identifying the stages, I continued to talk to women and men to determine if the assessments I had made were correct. Women who read through the stages quickly identified themselves as being in either Stage 1, 2, 3, or 4. I received the same response from men. They, too, were easily able to identify the category of their wives' behavior upon reading through the stages.

The information in *Women's Infidelity* is presented in the context of an ongoing conversation with Kevin (not his real name), a lifelong friend whom I consider a brother. Every incident that Kevin describes in the course of our nine meetings actually occurred. Everything I say in the book, I actually said, though sometimes in more casual terms than are appropriate for the printed page. Every bewildered, confused, angry, curious and insightful observation that Kevin makes in the book was actually shared, though not always in precisely the words recorded here.

Each of my meetings with Kevin is described in a separate chapter. While the chapter title suggests the primary theme of each conversation, various sub-themes are also developed. I have included a journal entry at the end of each chapter to summarize my insights and concerns following each meeting with Kevin.

I want to make clear that I am not claiming to be an expert. Ten years ago when I began to look for answers, I had only one goal: to understand what I was feeling. My interest continued long after my questions were answered simply because I found it fascinating that something so prevalent could be kept so secret. My purpose in writing *Women's Infidelity* is to share what I have learned. If the information in this book helps just one person or reduces even slightly the use of shame as a sexual deterrent for females, it will be worth every minute of the two years I spent writing it.

Chapter 1

Are Women Naturally Monogamous?

Hey, I need to talk to you.

Sure, what's up?

Tracey told me she doesn't know if she wants to be married anymore. She's talking about a separation.

Oh no, Kevin. I'm so sorry. What's going on? Did she tell you why?

No! She won't tell me anything. She just keeps saying that she's not happy, but every time I ask her why she's not happy, she says that she doesn't know. I don't know what to do. You know how much I love Tracey. We have always had a really good marriage. I just don't understand what's going on with her. God, I never thought I would be calling you about this. Tell me what I'm missing here. What's going on with her? Why is she doing this?

I'm not sure I'm going to be able to tell you anything that you really want to hear.

I'm not asking you to tell me what I want to hear. I'm asking you to tell me the *truth*. If you know what's going on with my wife, then tell me.

I can't know for sure what's going on with Tracey, but I have an idea what *could be* going on. But like I said, there's really no way to know for sure.

Then just tell me what you think it could be.

Kevin, Tracey is thirty-two years old. Marriage can be…kind of hard for women at that age.

Why is that?

Because at that age women are entering or already in their sexual prime.

No, that's not it. You don't understand. That doesn't have *anything* to do with what's going on with Tracey. She doesn't even like sex, so that can't be it.

Kevin, do you remember what it was like when you were in your sexual prime?

Yeah, I remember.

Do you remember wanting to have sex with one woman, or did you want to have sex with lots of women?

Now, what do you think? All guys want to have sex with *lots* of women.

What was it like back then, when you did have sex with just one woman. You know, for a long period of time?

It was difficult.

Okay, let me try to explain this to you by using your first marriage as a comparison. When you were married to Jill, you cheated on her, right?

Oh, come on. Why are you bringing that up? That's not any kind of a comparison. I was just young and stupid back then. I didn't know what was important. I was a dumb kid.

Were you really just young and stupid, or were you actually young, stupid, and horny?

Well, yeah. There is no denying that. I was horny all the time. I wanted to sleep with every woman I saw back then.

Except maybe one.

Who was that?

Jill. Don't you remember? Didn't you sort of lose interest in having sex with Jill?

Yeah, I remember.

How did you handle it? When that happened what did you do?

Well, obviously I didn't handle it. I just started cheating on Jill, that's all. But I told you I was stupid then.

Kevin, your wife is in her sexual prime and she is probably experiencing feelings similar to the ones you experienced when you were in your sexual prime. Somewhere around the late twenties and early thirties, a woman's body chemistry starts to change and the testosterone in her body becomes a little more potent, so to speak. That's why women seem to become more independent, aggressive and a little hairier as they get older. It's also quite common for them to experience a dramatic increase in their desire for other men.

Unless women change sexual partners, or as you guys like to say, get some "strange," they may lose interest in having sex with their current partner. They start getting that...you know...brother-sister feeling.

Ah, now I think I see what you're saying.

Unfortunately your wife's disinterest in sex has probably caused an increase in your desire to have sex with her.

You're right about that. Sometimes that's all I can think about. It drives me crazy.

You know it's natural for people to want what they think they can't have. It's a tendency we all share. In your sales work, you take advantage of that natural tendency all the time. You're always talking about the type of sales techniques you use to get people to buy things. I have heard you talk about the "take away" close, the "qualitative" close, the "negative" close. All those techniques are designed to make the buyer think they might not be able to get the product, which, as you know, automatically makes them want it. When I was in the weight-loss business, we used to tell people not to start dieting until after their second visit, which was typically two to three days after they enrolled in the program. In other words, they could eat whatever they wanted for two or three days. People would almost always come back for their second visit having lost weight. Their desire to eat would decrease just from knowing they could eat whatever they wanted.

Yeah, but this isn't my job. We're talking about my marriage. It's not like this is some kind of game.

Actually it's exactly like a game. And since nobody ever talks about it, we continue playing the game over and over again in our relationships. The reason people want what they can't have is because it's instinctive; we are genetically wired that way. That's why your sales techniques are so effective and it's also why you can't stop thinking about having sex with your wife right now.

I don't necessarily think that's true. My marriage doesn't boil down to a game.

Most of us don't like to think of our relationships as game-like, but just because we resist the idea doesn't mean that it's not a valid analogy. If we weren't caught up in a game-like pattern, we probably wouldn't keep doing the same thing over and over again.

Okay, so let's suppose this is what's going on with me and Tracey. What do I need to do?

I can't tell you what to do. I can only share with you the information I have gathered.

I know you can't tell me what to do, but right now I'm looking for answers. I need you to tell me everything you know about this.

Well, I'm warning you right now, it's going to take awhile because it's complicated.

Tracey and the kids are the most important things in my life and I don't care how long it takes. I want to figure this thing out.

Okay, here goes Kevin.

What many people don't know is that as men and women age, their body chemistries change. Sexually, men start becoming a little more like women and women start becoming a little more like men.

What? What the hell does that mean?

The changes are very subtle and gradual, but hormonal changes begin somewhere around the thirties in both sexes.

I don't believe that.

I want to read a few things to you from one of my books, which explains the process. In *The Alchemy of Love and Lust*, the author, Dr. Crenshaw, writes, "As a woman gets older she usually manifests more traditionally 'masculine' traits—decisiveness, assertiveness, physical sexuality, and independence. Men expand their 'female' dimension of touching, tenderness, insight, patience, and understanding." Later she writes, "Just as men are coming around, women in their thirties start heading in the opposite direction... subtle shifts have begun to occur in her (woman's) hormonal balance, enabling testosterone to manifest its influence more prominently. In general, her hormones are making her less reticent and more proactive in going after what she wants... A woman doesn't necessarily confront her spouse with her needs, or ask him for what she wants. She might go elsewhere. Orgasm gets the lion's share of her attention now."

Toward the end of her book, Dr. Crenshaw writes, "Our sexual distinctions (men's and women's) are almost indistinguishable at the beginning of our life and then again at the end ...As men and women age, their distinct characteristics begin to merge... the enzymatic activity in men slowly shifts to that more characteristic of women...Similarly, the hormone profile of a postmenopausal woman... is closer to that of the male than it has ever been during her lifetime..."[1]

Okay, first, you tell me my wife wants to screw other men and now you're telling me that I'm gradually turning into a woman. You were right, I'm not sure I want to hear this. I can't believe I have never heard anything about this before.

You're not turning into a woman. Men and women just become more alike as they age. But, like you, most people probably haven't heard anything about this. That's why the onset of the process can be extremely confusing and ultimately quite destructive for women who are already married.

Why do you say it can be destructive?

Because, a) women don't know it's coming, and b) women have been taught things about themselves that simply are not true.

Like what?

Namely, that they're naturally monogamous.

Are you saying that women *aren't* naturally monogamous?

Yes, that's exactly what I'm saying. On some level you must realize that we teach girls this myth in order to control their sexual behavior.

I guess maybe we do that, but I kind of thought it was true.

You didn't have to teach your daughters to pee, did you? You only had to teach them where you wanted them to pee. We don't have to teach people inherent behavior. We wouldn't spend so much time *telling* girls that they're naturally monogamous if they really were.

Then why do we teach them that in the first place?

Out of habit. We are still trying to control their sexual behavior. We haven't realized that teaching the myth to girls—or boys for that matter—is no longer necessary..

I'm not really sure I understand this. Why would we have taught something that wasn't really true to begin with?

So men could ease their insecurity about paternity.

Oh, come on...

Until recently, men had no way of knowing if offspring were genetically theirs. Males of other species use all kinds of techniques to increase the chances of their sperm fertilizing the female's egg, not the sperm of another male. Mating naturally triggers anxiety in males. For males, uncertainty is part of the reproductive process.[2]

Reproduction was the one contest in which men had no interest in competing because, like I said, until recently men could never really know who the winners were.

In order to ease their insecurity and ensure the perpetuation of their genes, men claimed women as property and demanded their fidelity. Female survival was contingent upon marriage, but marriage was contingent upon virginity.[3] Female infidelity was unacceptable to the degree that incidents of infidelity could be punishable by death. Surely you are aware that even today in some countries little girls are circumcised to curtail their sexual desire and females can be punished or killed for having premarital or extramarital sex. Hasn't it ever occurred to you that we spend a lot of energy attempting to keep females from having sex? If you think women are naturally monogamous, hasn't it ever seemed odd to you, or at the very least like a big waste of time to resort to such drastic measures if females are not likely to be unfaithful anyway?

I guess I just never thought about it. I mean...what you're saying does makes sense.

Virginity is revered, and in some places *required* for females prior to marriage, because in the past it was the only way men could ease their paternal insecurity. Since we now have tests that can determine paternity with certainty, perpetuating the belief that females are naturally monogamous is no longer necessary. In fact, in our society, it may be doing more harm than good.

Why do you say that?

Because young females are conditioned to believe that they are naturally monogamous and they carry this belief with them throughout their lifetimes. So when women experience feelings that deviate from this belief, particularly after they are married, those feelings can cause enormous internal conflict. Many women resolve the dilemma by dissolving their marriages.

Some women find it easier to think they married the wrong guy than to see themselves as some sort of shameful freak of nature. Their erroneous belief in a monogamous predisposition prevents them from becoming aware of their natural sexual tendencies in the first place. This unawareness can cause a chain reaction that ultimately destroys their marriages. What I'm trying to tell you is, your wife's body may just be wanting something different, or as you probably call it, wanting some "strange."

Women want "strange?"

Yes, but many women don't know it, because they have been conditioned to believe that they are naturally monogamous. However, it makes sense that women would become more desirous of multiple sexual partners during their sexual prime, since testosterone is having a greater influence on their bodies.

It does make sense. I don't know why, but I always assumed that women had sex more frequently with their husbands during their sexual prime.

That's what you have been taught to believe, but it's also what you *want* to believe—even though your experiences have told you that it isn't necessarily true.

What do you mean by that?

Remember when you were twenty and you thought you were going to hell?

Which time?

When you were working at the hardware store and that older woman came in and asked you out?

Oh, that...yeah, I remember.

Wasn't she married and in her thirties?

Yeah, but I would never have slept with her if she'd told me she was married.

Why do think she didn't tell you until after you had sex?

I'm not stupid. I know she just wanted sex.

So, this woman comes into the hardware store, asks you out, takes you home and has sex with you in the bed she normally shares with her husband. And afterwards she tells you to hurry up and leave because her husband is coming home. Didn't you think that was odd behavior for someone who was supposed to be naturally monogamous?

At the time, all I cared about was whether or not I was going to hell for it. You know how I was brought up. That really tormented me for a long time.

You know, I've talked to a lot of men who have had similar experiences. One guy I talked to was only fourteen when his mother's best friend seduced him.

Lucky guy.

He wasn't lucky and you know it. It bothered him for years, just like sleeping with that married woman bothered you.

Your beliefs aren't allowing you to put two and two together.

What do you mean?

If I recall correctly, you were the person who warned me not to get too involved when I was seeing a considerably younger man. You said every young guy is with an older woman at least once. Didn't you tell me that having sex with an older woman is a right-of-passage for guys when they're young?

It is. Every man I know was with an older woman at least once when he was younger.

And how many of those men found out they were with married women?

Some were married women, but some were divorced or separated.

You had sex with a woman who was separated, didn't you?

Yeah.

Didn't she go back to her husband?

She did.

How many times did you have sex with her?

We had sex nonstop for about three days.

On day four, did she decide she was going back to her husband?

That's pretty much what happened.

She may not have been separated at all. Her husband may have been out of town and she just wanted some "strange."

No, she was separated from the guy. She told me about some of the problems they were having. Her husband really didn't treat her very well and he didn't pay any attention to her.

"My spouse doesn't pay attention to me," is code for "I need some 'strange.'" How many married people approach potential sex partners with, "Hey, my marriage is great. I'm just kind of bored right now and I would like to have sex with somebody different. Are you in?" How often do you think that happens?

I don't get it, though. Why would a woman have to lie? Women can get laid anytime they want.

Are you kidding? You already said that had you known the woman who came into the store was married you wouldn't have slept with her.

I wouldn't have, but I'm sure a lot of other guys would.

That's where you're wrong. For one thing, women in their late twenties and thirties are often sexually attracted to, and sexually compatible with, males who are in their late teens and early twenties, because both are in their sexual prime. The problem is, married women quickly find that young guys are morally opposed to sleeping with married women—just like you were. So some women may present themselves as single, or lie about their marital status. They may even claim to be separated when they go out looking for a one- or two-night stand.

You're saying this happens a lot?

You tell me. You said that you and every guy you know has been with an older woman and several of those women were married. It's like I said before, your beliefs aren't allowing you to put two and two together. You have known since you were a teenager that older women like sex, but just like every other man I have talked to, when told your wife is in her sexual prime, you say, "No...not my wife, you don't understand...my wife doesn't even like sex." I'm telling you, the husband of the woman who came into the hardware store and had sex with you at her house that night would probably have said the same thing about his wife.

Guys seem to think that a hundred or so women roam the planet providing recreational sex to millions of men, but I'm telling you that's not the case. One man's good girl just might be another man's bad girl.

Okay, I get it. How long is this shit going to last with my wife?

If you're asking about the changes in your wife's body chemistry, then the answer is the changes are going to continue. Women and men continue to become more similar as they age. But, if you're asking how long these changes are going to influence her behavior, the answer is: it depends. It's quite possible that your wife is completely unaware of what is causing any changes she might be experiencing. If so, she's likely to attribute her feelings to something else.

Like what?

If she's feeling a loss of sexual desire for you and increased sexual desire for other men, or has been with another man, she might be thinking she married the wrong guy.

Are you serious? Why would she think that? Why wouldn't she just see it for what it is—you know, a fling or something?

Kevin, you know the feeling you get when you first meet someone you're attracted to? That kind of buzzed, want-to-be-with-her-and-have-sex-all-the-time feeling?

Yeah.

If you had to name that feeling, what would you call it?

You mean infatuation...that's what you're talking about, right?

Most men I have talked to call it infatuation, but most of the women I have talked to call it being in love.

But it *is* infatuation. Why would women think it's anything else? Everybody knows that feeling wears off.

No, they don't. Many people today are looking for soul mates. They think if they find the right person, the intensity will last. Women in particular may believe that intense feelings can last. They've been taught to believe that they should only want sex with someone they love. So when a woman desires a man, she thinks she is in love, and when the desire fades she thinks she is out of love. Many men harbor the same illusion at some point in their lives.

I don't think guys ever confuse infatuation with love. We know that the feeling goes away.

Really? Wasn't it a woman that led to your divorce from Jill?

Do you remember everything? Why are you bringing that up?

As I recall, after you divorced Jill to be with Judy—you know, the woman you just couldn't live without—the relationship only lasted about a year.

Thanks for reminding me of that, but I was young. I didn't know any better back then. Now I know what I did was stupid.

Why do you think I don't screw around now? I learn from my mistakes.

Kevin, you weren't just stupid. You were young, horny, and high as a kite. Look, the feeling many women—and men—associate with "being in love" is actually due to a chemical that gets released in our brains when we are attracted to someone. The brain chemical is called *pheylethylamine*, or PEA for short. The feeling experienced when PEA is triggered in the brain is similar to the feeling one would experience after snorting cocaine. PEA is a euphoria-inducing stimulant.

Really?

Yes. The effects of PEA can last longer than stimulants that are ingested. And we have the ability to increase PEA levels with our thoughts.

How does that work?

Just thinking about a person can increase levels of PEA, which is why we spend so much time fantasizing about the people we are attracted to. It gives us a buzz. But, the more we're around the person, the less capable we are of experiencing the high we felt in the beginning of the relationship. Our bodies build up a tolerance to PEA, much as they do to some of the drugs we smoke, snort, or ingest. Also, as with drugs, PEA is addictive.

So if your wife is seeing someone, she may think she's in love with the guy, but in actuality she may be addicted to the high she gets from being around him and from thinking about him.

If this is really what's going on with Tracey, what can I do to stop it?

Kevin, I want to ask you something, and when I ask, please don't think I'm trying to be cruel. I just want to help you understand.

Ask me.

Was there anything that your first wife could have done to keep you from leaving her?

That hurts.

I didn't ask the question to make you feel bad. I'm trying to help you understand. So, can you tell me, what could your first wife have done to prevent your leaving?

Nothing. There wasn't anything anyone could do. Now, I don't know what to do. I don't want my daughters to have to go through all that pain that my son went through when I left him and his mom. I still think about what I put them through.

Kevin, I know that you still grieve over the breakup and that you didn't intend to hurt anyone. You simply didn't understand what you were feeling at the time. We call it being in love, but it would be more accurate if instead we called it being "on love," because it's not very different from being on a drug. In the book *Mean Genes*, the authors say, "… drugs generally mimic chemicals used by our body during normal functioning."[4]

The chemicals in our body are similar to drugs. Particular behaviors lead to specific increases or "shots" of certain chemicals in the brain. The two chemicals involved in the sensation we call *love* are similar to cocaine and heroin. The feeling we experience at the beginning of a relationship is a combination of being hyper, excited and euphoric. We lose our appetite and don't need as much sleep. We feel as though we've found the key to the universe. We fantasize and obsess over the person we are attracted to. I remember when I met my husband, I used to fantasize about how awesome domesticity would be. I actually daydreamed about doing his laundry and washing our dishes.

You? That's hard to believe.

Embarrassingly, I did. The feeling of being in love is similar to the feeling produced by snorting cocaine. I have a theory that under certain circumstances—such as an affair—some people experience a feeling that is closer to the high produced by smoking crack—a higher high, so to speak. But we can talk about my theories later.

The feeling we experience after the high, which occurs naturally if we are frequently and consistently with the same person, is called *attachment*. It's the bondedness that you experience with Tracey. But unlike attraction, which is similar to the feelings we get from amphetamines, attachment is more like a narcotic—morphine or heroin, for example. Narcotics give us a relaxed, comfortable feeling. Living with someone, or seeing someone regularly for a long period of time, causes the release of chemicals in our bodies. It happens naturally and without our knowing it, but it's comparable to getting regular shots of heroin or morphine. This is the feeling many people call, "true love," or "real love." It's also similar to the bond you share with your kids.

I know this information isn't going to change the way you feel right now, but perhaps it will give you some idea of what might be going on with Tracey—and you.

A few years ago I wrote a twenty-page information booklet. The booklet is a combination of information I compiled from books and interviews with women and men. Throughout my research, which largely entailed listening to women discuss feelings about their marriages, I felt as though I was hearing different parts of the same story told over and over again. I identified distinctive patterns and behaviors that I later began to view as stages women experience during the course of long-term relationships.

I want to e-mail you a section of the booklet that describes these stages. After reading through the four stages, you can determine whether you think Tracey falls into one of them. And, if you like, we can get together one day next week and talk about this some more.

You know I really appreciate this...

I know you do, but it's really no problem. I probably spend five to ten hours a week talking about this to people I don't even know.

I'll talk to you soon.

The Information Sent to Kevin

Stage 1

At this stage, the women I interviewed said that they felt as though something was missing in their lives. They had all the things that they wanted—a home, a family, a great husband—but felt they should be happier. Over time, many of the women noticed a distinct loss of sexual desire; they reported that they were no longer interested in sex. They spent a great deal of energy trying to avoid physical contact with their husbands for fear it might lead to a sexual encounter. They frequently complained of physical ailments to avoid having sex and often tried to avoid going to bed at the same time as their husbands. They viewed sex as a job, not unlike doing the dishes or going to the grocery store. Some of the women claimed that when their husbands touched them, they felt violated; they said their bodies would freeze up and they would feel tightness in their chest and/or a sick feeling in their stomach. The majority of the women in Stage 1 felt there was something wrong with them, that they were in some way defective. They were also fearful that their disinterest in sex would cause their husbands to cheat, or worse yet, leave them.

Stage 2

Women at Stage 2 experienced reawakened desire stimulated by encounters outside the marital relationship. Whether the new relationships involved sex or remained platonic, they were emotionally significant to these women.

Many of the women had felt no sexual desire for a long time. Many experienced tremendous guilt and regret, regardless of whether their new relationships were sexual, merely emotional, or both. Most experienced what could be termed an identity crisis—even those who tried to put the experience behind them. Constant reminders were everywhere. They felt guilt when the topic of infidelity arose, whether in the media, in conversations with family and friends, or at home with their husbands. They could no longer express their prior disdain for infidelity without feeling like hypocrites. They felt as though they had lost a part of themselves. Reflecting society's belief that women are either "good" or "bad," these women questioned their "good girl" status and felt that they might not be deserving of their husbands. Many tried to overcome feelings of guilt by becoming more attentive toward and appreciative of their husbands. However, over time the predominant reaction of a number of the women moved from appreciation to justification. In order to justify their continued desire for other men, they began to attribute those desires to needs that were not being met in the marriage, or to their husband's past behavior. Many became negative and sarcastic when speaking of their husbands and their marriages. In many cases, an extramarital affair soon followed.

Stage 3

Women at Stage 3 were involved in affairs, ending affairs, or contemplating divorce. The women who were having affairs said that their feelings were unlike anything they'd experienced before. They felt "alive" again and many believed that they had found their soul mates. These women were experiencing feelings associated with a chemically altered state, or what we typically refer to as being in love.

These women also talked of being in tremendous pain, the pain of choosing between their husbands and their new love interests. They believed that what they were doing was wrong and unfair to their husbands, but were unable to end their affairs. Many tried several times. Prior to meeting with their lovers, they would vow that this would be the last time, but were unable to stick with their decisions.

Unable to end their extramarital relationships, the women concluded that their lovers were soul mates. Unaware that they had become addicted to the high caused by chemicals released during the initial stages of a relationship, they were unable to choose. Many lived in a state of limbo for years. "Should I stay married or should I get a divorce?" was the question continuously on their minds. Some of the women attempted to initiate separations. In most cases, their husbands launched futile attempts to make their wives happy by being more attentive, spending more time at home and helping out around the house. Regardless of these women's past and present complaints, the last thing they wanted was to spend more time with their husbands. Many women successfully gained separations.

The reason many gave for separating was a "search for self." They convinced their husbands that they might be able to save the marriage if they could just have time to themselves. They continued to tell their husbands that time apart was the only hope of improving the current situation. Several of these women said they wanted to free themselves of the restrictions of marriage and spend more time with their lovers. Most thought that eventually their confusion would disappear and they would know with certainty that they either wanted to stay married or get divorced in order to be with their lovers. By separating, these women were able to enjoy the high experienced with their new partners without letting go of the security of their marriages. The husbands were still unaware that their wives were having affairs. Their lack of suspicion was due in part to their wife's disinterest in sex and their belief that she was a "good girl."

Several women at this stage were ending an extramarital affair. In most cases, it was not their decision. The majority were involved with single men who either lost interest because the relationship could not progress or were attracted to other women who were, in most cases, single. The women whose affairs were ending experienced extreme grief, became deeply depressed and expressed tremendous anger toward their husbands. Unaware that they were experiencing chemical withdrawal due to sudden changes in brain chemistry, many felt that they had missed their chance at happiness due to their own indecisiveness.

However, these women did not return to their husbands, at least not emotionally. Believing they had become more aware of what they wanted and needed from a mate, many placed the utmost importance on finding a relationship that gave them the feeling they experienced in their affairs. To these women a new relationship with a new partner represented a clean slate, a chance to regain their "good girl" status. Some searched for new partners during their separations. Others returned to their marriages, but still continued to search. Some women resumed sporadic sexual relations with their husbands in an effort to safeguard the marriage until they made a decision. Although most were not sexually attracted to their husbands, desire was temporarily rekindled when they suspected their husbands were unfaithful, were contemplating infidelity, or when their husbands showed signs of moving on.

Stage 4

The women in stage four included those who chose to stay married and continue their affairs and those who chose to divorce. Some of the women who continued their affairs stated that marital sex was improved by maintaining the extramarital relationship. Some thought the lover was a soul mate, but for one reason or another did not leave their husband and did not feel torn between the two. Others realized that their feelings were intensified by not sharing day-to-day living arrangements with their lover. Almost all of the women in this latter category were having affairs with married men. They believed their affairs could continue indefinitely without disrupting either partner's primary relationship.

The women who chose divorce and were in the beginning stages of a new relationship typically expressed relief at having finally made a decision and reported feeling normal again. Many of the divorced women who had remarried and were several years into their new marriages seemed somewhat reluctant to talk about the specifics of their past experiences. However, they did mention feelings of guilt and regret for having hurt their children and ex-spouses only to find themselves experiencing similar feelings in the new relationship.

June 19, 2003

I hope I'm wrong about what I think is going on with Tracey, but from my experience when a woman says, "I'm not happy," what she really means is, "I'm bored, and/or horny." And when a woman follows up with, "I think we should separate," what she really means is, "I'm sleeping with somebody else," or "I want to sleep with somebody else." I'm still amazed at how common and predictable this behavior is in women.

Chapter 2

The Sexual Devaluing System

I'm sorry I didn't call before stopping by, but I need to talk to you. I read the information you sent me and it sounds like Tracey is in Stage 3. I don't know what to do. I'm just so damned mad right now. I swear I feel like killing somebody.

I know.

How do other people feel when you tell them this stuff?

It depends on whether I'm talking to a man or a woman. Women are typically relieved and say it's nice to know that they're normal. Men are usually initially relieved, but then they tend to vacillate between feelings of empathy and anger. I know you're scared right now. The thought of Tracey leaving has got to be scary as hell. It's natural to feel that way.

I don't remember being scared since I was a kid, but you're right, I don't know what I will do if Tracey leaves me.

I know it will be difficult for you. When my marriage was ending, I didn't understand why, even though I wanted to get divorced, for some reason I just couldn't. The thought of not having my husband there for me when I needed him made me panicky. For a period of time after we separated, I became anxious when I did not see or talk to my husband for more than a couple of days. The feeling I was having was similar to the feeling children get when they are separated from their parents. It's that losing-your-mom-in-a-department-store feeling. I experienced the same feeling intermittently throughout my separation. I was experiencing what is often referred to as separation anxiety. Remember, when we are attached to someone, we get a safe, comfortable feeling from being around them. When we are separated from that person, it's like going through a narcotic withdrawal. That's the reason we become anxious or panicky.

Do you think it would help if I gave Tracey that stuff you wrote about the stages?

In my opinion, it would only help if Tracey were in Stage 1 or 2, the "I'm bored," or "I screwed up" stage. But, after reading the stages, you think Tracey is in Stage 3, and I would have to agree with you. Her desire to separate is an indication that someone else is probably involved. In other words, Tracey is probably in the grip of a very powerful addiction.

Try to remember how you felt in your first marriage. You were torn between your attachment to Jill and your attraction to Judy. Those feelings had chemical origins. It was like trying to decide between an addiction to heroin, which your frequent contact with Jill provided, and a subsequent addiction to cocaine, which your new and infrequent contact with Judy provided.

I'm not sure your telling me all this is helping. I'm feeling more and more like an ass for what I did in my first marriage. I'm also beginning to think that there's nothing I can do to prevent Tracey from doing the same thing to me.

If Tracey is seeing someone, she is going to have to go through a withdrawal period, either from you or from the other guy, which may be why she wants to separate instead of just getting a divorce. People separate not just to see if the grass is greener. Some don't believe they can stop seeing the new person, so they try to find out if they can live without the old person. How was it with you? Did you really want to divorce Jill, or did you want to stay married and continue seeing Judy?

I wanted them both. This is so screwed up. I can't believe I'm going to have to go through this again.

You're *not* going through the same thing again. This time you are experiencing what Jill went through.

Did you have to point that out? I know I deserve this.

Kevin, I don't think for a minute that you deserve this—or that anyone does, for that matter. Getting divorced or separated can be more difficult than dealing with a spouse's death, yet nobody talks about it. This is one of the most painful experiences that any of us can go through, but we keep pretending that having good morals or finding the right person will prevent it from happening.

But I knew it could happen. That's why I made a conscious decision never to cheat on Tracey.

I don't want to take anything away from you, but your resolve to be faithful in this marriage may have something to do with hormonal changes that are occurring in *your* body. I know you made a conscious decision to be faithful this time, but like I tried to explain to you the other day, it was probably your past experiences *combined* with bodily changes that enabled you to decide.

Society makes it difficult for women to make a conscious decision about marriage, let alone fidelity. Girls have always been taught from a young age that men do not want to marry women who have been with numerous sexual partners. At the same time, we entice girls with romantic notions surrounding meeting the right man, getting married and living happily ever after. Many women end up denying and/or suppressing their natural sexual desires in order to get married.

These two beliefs are taught simultaneously to girls and they are the cause of many women's high and unrealistic expectations of marriage. Men, on the other hand, are taught that marriage is definitely something they'll want to postpone. Marriage for men means loss of freedom and a reduction in sexual partners. So men have a lower expectation of marriage from the beginning. Women are more likely to be let down by marriage; it just isn't as great as they thought it was going to be. But men may find that it's better than they thought, since many of them had expected it to suck in the first place. Men have nowhere to go but up and women have nowhere to go but down due to their preconceived expectations.

I understand what you're saying, but I don't see how society could have enough of an influence on girls to convince

them that they don't like to screw around. No one could have convinced me of that.

With the right motivation and with the threat of repercussions, don't bet on it.

But we don't punish females for having sex.

The use of shame as a sexual deterrent for girls is as prevalent today as it was in the past. Let's go into my office. I want to read something to you.

Recently Dr. Phil did a show called, "Teens and Sex." Early in the program, Dr. Phil began citing statistics. He said, "Ten percent of teens will have sex by age thirteen. Fifty percent of all kids are sexually active by the time they reach the tenth grade. One in five sexually active girls gets pregnant in high school. Half of all teens don't believe that oral sex is sex. So what a-- we're gonna do today is talk to you to make sure it isn't your daughter."

Judging from Dr. Phil's introduction, a viewer could easily conclude that the problem isn't teen sex, it's girls having sex.

Later in the show, Dr. Phil once again announced the show's topic. He said, "Our topic is 'Teens and Sex' and what effect it has on them. Teens have no idea of the emotional ramifications involved in having any type of sex. And that's what we're talking about…how to prevent your daughter from having oral sex that first time, how to get her to understand that if you choose the action, you choose the consequences."

Again, the audience heard the same discrepancy between the show's topic and the host's actual words. Teens don't experience consequences, girls do.

The show included a tape of Dr. Phil's son, Jay, interviewing girls and boys about how they felt after having had sex. He asked a boy, "And if you go out to a party and you meet a girl for the first time and you have oral sex with her-- and that's happened, right? Did you look at her any differently?" The boy said, "Like, if she'll give you oral sex that easily, what makes you think she wouldn't do that with every other guy? So, yea, I'd think she's a slut."

I don't think you understand. That's the way guys think…

Don't you see? That boy probably doesn't even know why he thinks that way. By engaging in oral sex, he eliminates the chance of pregnancy from his sexual encounters. Nonetheless, he is unconsciously plagued with paternity insecurity, a fear and an insecurity that has been passed down to him by generation after generation of men who could never be certain about paternity.

These illusionary insecurities cause males to be disinterested in girls who are sexually willing. Many boys and men feel that they can ease this insecurity by either finding females who would like to have sex but don't, thereby exhibiting self-control, or in finding females that appear to be disinterested in sex altogether. These fears are fears from the past, a past that did not include DNA testing. Uncertainty no longer has to be a part of the reproduction process for males.

What you're saying makes sense, but I still don't think guys can make girls *not* have sex just because they don't want them to.

Yes they can. That's not all that was said on the show that day. When Jay was interviewing the girls, a couple of them said they regretted having had sex, so he asked one of them, "...Why do you regret it?" The girl replied, "Because you just feel horrible that you just lost something that you can't ever get back. And I think I did it for the wrong reasons...I was a disappointment to my grandma and that I disappointed myself because I know I wanted to wait longer. If I could go back, I would probably wait on having sex." This girl then appeared on the show and talked to Dr. Phil in person.

Dr. Phil began by saying, "Now you're being raised by your grandmother, right? ...And I think we can agree that she's doing a pretty good job. You're doing well in school...You're a varsity golfer, you play basketball at school. You're in good shape. You're doing good academically. You're life is working along well...But you sold out in this area." She replied, "Yes."

Dr. Phil then said, "How do you feel about that?" She said, "I feel like I could have waited. Like I got nothing out of this. Like it didn't help me in any way, that I'm a disappointment to myself that I didn't—I couldn't resist temptation and it wasn't all it was cracked up to be."

Dr. Phil then asked the girl to think about something that she was proud of. After she recounted an experience in which she felt proud of herself, Dr. Phil said, "Compare that to how you felt when you got up from having oral sex." Moments later, Dr. Phil said to the girl, "I want you to do something for me. Stand up. I want you to look at that camera right there. You have no idea how many young girls in America are watching you right now. And I want you to save them the hell you've been through. I want you to tell them right now, 'Don't you do it. Don't you sell out.'"

Through tears, the girl stood in front of the camera and said, "Don't do it. Don't sell out because you're worth much more than that. Cause you're not going to feel any better about yourself by doing it. You're going to feel so low and you're going to regret it. And you're going to lose all the self-respect that you have for yourself. If you say 'no,' you're going to feel like the best person in the world and you're going to have the greatest high that you can ever get."

I was so upset after watching that show, in my opinion instead of "Teens and Sex," the topic of the show should have been "Emotional Stoning." It was something that could possibly be beneficial if aired in less civilized societies. The teasers for the show could have been, "Eliminate the need for female circumcision and stoning. Use emotional stoning, it's an effective sexual deterrent for girls of all ages."

I can't believe that really happened…that sucks.

I know. It broke my heart. Unfortunately, programs about teens and sex typically fail to acknowledge the female sex drive. The differences between what males and females find sexually pleasurable is usually not discussed. Instead, girls are simply advised not to have sex.

It really doesn't seem fair.

Females say that it's not fair all the time. They're envious of the sexual freedom that males have, which should tell you something.

And that is?

Let me put it this way. In order to feel envy, you have to be desirous of something that someone else has. If males were the only sex of the species to get cancer, females wouldn't be envious of males for it. They wouldn't be wishing they could get it too.

The reality is, the young girl on Dr. Phil's show probably felt as though she had lost something because we lead girls to believe that they are *worth less* after they have sex. If society rewarded girls for having sex, her experience would have been completely different. Couple the shame she feels with the likelihood that she did not have an orgasm, and it becomes clear why she probably felt like she lost something, and also why she felt she didn't get anything out of it. Physiologically, females lose nothing from having sex—they actually gain something. It's common knowledge that nature intended males to spread their seed. I think what most people don't realize is that nature also intended females to gather it.

Let me read something to you from one of the books I quoted when we talked the other day. In *Mean Genes,* the authors say, "...In humans about 99% of the sperm in an ejaculation are not fertile at all. Many of the non-fertile sperm are "seek-and-destroy" sperm that actively search for the sperm of other men and annihilate them, while others function as blockers, denying other men's sperm access to the uterus."[1]

Males wanted and needed females to be monogamous; however, it doesn't appear that that's what nature had in mind. Unfortunately though, we continue to teach females that their worth is tied to their sexuality. In our society, the valuing system used in the automobile industry is remarkably similar to the valuing system we apply to women's sexual behavior.

Female virginity is equal to the value of a new car—the loss of virginity is the equivalent of driving a new car off the lot. Each additional sexual partner is about the equivalent of ten-thousand miles. When a girl's sexual partners reach the double digits, it's similar to the value of a car that's odometer has turned over.

That's a pretty good analogy. I don't think I have ever heard it put like that before.

Well, in response to this *devaluing* system, females have adopted anti-mileage techniques such as, "everything but intercourse" and "old boyfriend sex." These techniques are effective because mileage only accrues when females have intercourse with a new partner. Females can have sex every day, all day long with the same partner and not accumulate additional miles.

For some females the fear of losing value is so strong that it can cause them to continue in either abusive or unsatisfying relationships.

Don't you think this could be one of the reasons that females appear to want commitment? Since girls and boys are taught early on about the female sexual valuing system, isn't it only logical that females would want commitment before and after they have sex, given that every new partner diminishes their value in the marital market place? When you take into consideration the fact that young girls are taught that marriage is their ultimate goal, it becomes obvious why secrecy and lies continue to be a part of female sexuality. Lying enables females to roll back their odometers and regain value, while anti-mileage techniques enable them to experience the pleasure of orgasms without losing their value.

What exactly are you talking about when you say women can have orgasms without losing value?

Clitoral stimulation, as opposed to vaginal stimulation, is what brings most females to orgasm. When females are young, they are naturally inclined to desire clitoral stimulation through masturbation, not through intercourse. Since intercourse doesn't lead most girls to orgasm, they are likely to find the experience frustrating or painful, rather than pleasurable. Many girls initially engage in intercourse because boys tell them how good it's going to feel. Many girls agree to have intercourse because they assume that intercourse, which for most young females will not result in orgasm, will feel even better than oral sex or being masturbated by their boyfriends, which may have already resulted in orgasm.

After experiencing the letdown of intercourse, "clitoral girls," as I call them, may continue to allow boys to touch and stroke them to orgasm, although they often hide their pleasure. They don't let their male partners know that they are having orgasms. In fact, during intimate encounters, they often pretend that they want to have intercourse but are resisting temptation. The resistance is in many cases an act, not a testament to their self-control. The practice of faking *not* having orgasms is as much a part of female sexuality as faking *having* them.

By appearing to resist something they desire—intercourse—clitoral girls find themselves planted firmly in society's good-girl category. It can be a win-win situation for them: good girl status and orgasms.

I guess that's why girls will let guys do everything but fuck them.

You would do the same thing if every time you slept with a different girl you lost ten-thousand dollars. Don't you think you would limit your sexual partners, lie about the ones you did have and find ways to have orgasms without losing your cash?

Although the majority of young females fall into this category, there are some girls who easily achieve orgasm through intercourse. "Vaginal girls," as I call them, may not feel sexually satisfied without having intercourse. Vaginal girls are more likely to engage in intercourse and less likely to feel that they don't get anything out of the experience. Needless to say, maintaining virtue and avoiding the accumulation of mileage can be much more difficult for vaginal girls.

When I was in high school, I thought I was in love with this girl named Sheri. But she gave me a blow job and we ended up having sex on our first date, so I never asked her out again. I know this sounds stupid, but because of the way I was brought up, I just couldn't imagine the mother of my children giving me a blow job, especially on the first date.

Well then, the good news is you got what you wanted. The mother of your children doesn't give you blow jobs.

Try to remember you're supposed to be helping.

Kevin, the way you reacted towards Sheri is exactly what teaches females to lie and pretend to be something they're not. You saw her as a bad girl. If she waited to have sex with the next guy she dated, he would have viewed her as a good girl, but the only change would have been her ability to manipulate a male's perception of her.

Females utilize a number of methods to postpone having sex. They wear ugly underwear or intentionally don't shave their legs and pubic hair so they won't have to rely on their willpower. Females even use their periods to help them appear virtuous to males. If a menstruating woman meets a man she likes and wants to have sex with, she tells the man she wants to wait to have sex. She doesn't tell him it's because she's menstruating. She says it's because she isn't ready to have sex yet. The man ends up thinking the woman is not "that kind of girl." The woman appears virtuous to the man just because she happens to be having her period when they meet.

When I was a teenager, I had a girlfriend who was a vaginal girl. She only enjoyed having orgasms from intercourse. She didn't have the luxury of choice that clitoral girls enjoy; she needed to have intercourse to feel sexually fulfilled. I remember having a conversation with her when we were both about sixteen. She had been dating a guy and they had just broken up. She was really bummed out one night and said, "I wish we were older. When we're older sex won't be such a big deal. It will be okay for us to have sex then, won't it?" She had already had sex with three guys and she knew she was losing value. My friend hated having to play the game; she thought it was ridiculous. She liked sex and she didn't enjoy pretending that she didn't. I realize now that the difference between our perception of girls that do and girls that don't may just be due to variances in their chemistries and physical makeup as opposed to willpower and morality. In many cases, good girls are just girls that aren't naturally inclined to want to have intercourse yet.

I think most guys know that girls and women lie about how many guys they've slept with.

I agree. Most guys probably do think females lie about the number of partners they've had, but I don't think guys realize that females also lie to themselves. They try *not* to remember how many guys they've slept with because it's painful for them; it makes them feel worthless. So they try to disassociate themselves from some of their sexual experiences. Several women told me their "real" number of sexual partners was different than the number they admitted to. Many of the women I interviewed said they had certain criteria that determined whether a sexual experience counted in their eyes, because counting all sexual experiences made them feel bad about themselves.

I want to go back to something we were talking about before. A minute ago you were talking about girls and, I assume

women too, being either vaginal or clitoral. Some females can have orgasms both ways, right?

Yes, some females are able to experience orgasms by messing around *and* during intercourse. They're called lucky girls.

As females age though, their body chemistry changes and they eventually enter a stage where thrusting and vaginal stimulation are desired. This happens during a woman's sexual peak. Intercourse becomes more desirable for females even if it doesn't lead to orgasm; their bodies want thrusting just like young girls who have higher levels of testosterone.

I want to go back and ask about something you said earlier. You said females pretend that they don't have orgasms when they really do. Are you saying that sometimes my wife might pretend that she didn't have an orgasm when she did? I'm not sure I understand. Why would a woman pretend that she *didn't* have an orgasm? I can't understand why my wife or any other woman would do that.

It's not something your wife would do with you. It's something a girl or woman does with a new partner.

But, why? I don't get it.

Because intercourse with a new partner is costly for females. Since females achieve orgasms through clitoral stimulation, why would they be willing to lower their value by proceeding on to intercourse? Put yourself in the same situation. If you could achieve an orgasm through oral sex, why pay ten-thousand dollars to have intercourse? Unlike a female, though, you wouldn't be able to hide your orgasm.

But why would I want to?

Reverse the situation. Let's say a girl wants to have intercourse with you because it not only gives her pleasure, but her ego is boosted every time she sleeps with a new partner. If society promoted the notion that having intercourse with as many boys as possible was womanly, she would be trying to talk you into having intercourse. However, assuming that intercourse costs you money, you will probably prefer to have an orgasm from oral stimulation. Don't you think this girl will eventually become angry because you are having orgasms and she isn't? Or, even if she is having orgasms, they aren't feeding her ego. She isn't proving her womanliness by societal standards.

By pretending not to have orgasms, which females can easily do, they experience pleasure, accrue no mileage and keep males from being angry at them. Society has created a system where females are unable to share and enjoy sexual pleasure with males.

So, is this just something girls do? What about when women want intercourse? You know, when they're in their prime. They don't pretend they're not having orgasms anymore, right?

Not necessarily. Women can also use this method as a screening device. Let's say a woman meets a man she's attracted to. She may just mess around with him, have an orgasm, but decide against sleeping with him.

If she really wants to have intercourse, why would she decide not to?

Because after messing around with the guy, she might realize that intercourse with him is unlikely to be fulfilling.

You mean she thinks the guy won't be good in bed?

Exactly. During the messing around stage, she might discover that the guy has a small penis and decide to pass on intercourse. It just may not be worth the miles.

What, are you kidding me? A woman might decide not to sleep with a guy because he has a little dick?

You may want to believe that the size of a man's penis doesn't matter, but it can matter a lot—especially during a woman's sexual prime.

A few times during my research I was able to interview both partners in a relationship. I remember this thirty-six year old, very attractive divorced woman who had started seeing the recently promoted president of the bank where she worked. The guy was a twenty-nine year old, average looking, married man.

The guy was married?

Yeah, he was married and his wife was pregnant with their first child.

What an asshole.

Would it have been better if he had waited until his wife had the child and the child was older, like you did?

I'm not saying that…I just…

Kevin I'm not trying to make you feel bad. I am just trying to help you get it. Unless we stop judging people we're never going to understand this aspect of our behavior.

Go on with the story.

Anyway, this man and woman started out talking and flirting with each other, then began meeting for drinks. Over a period of three months, they talked about the possibility of him leaving his wife and the two of them starting a life together, but they didn't have sex—only kissed and fooled around. One night while they were together, the woman decided to give the guy oral sex and that's when she found out that he had a really small penis.

I can't believe that people tell you this kind of stuff.

I've found that people are pretty open about their experiences if you are interested in what they have to say and don't judge them.

After having oral sex with this guy the woman wasn't interested in him anymore. She said she knew that sex with him wouldn't be fulfilling.

She didn't tell the guy she didn't want to see him anymore because he had a little dick, did she?

No, unfortunately she didn't.

What do you mean unfortunately? No man wants to hear that. You don't know what that can do to a guy's self-esteem.

I think I do. It probably makes a man feel the same way a woman feels after she has a child and her vagina has stretched out, or the way many women feel when they start getting older and believe they are no longer sexually desirable to men. Don't think these things affect a woman's self-esteem any less than they affect a man's. Society has just always been more protective of male self-esteem.

Well what happened, what did she tell the guy?

She told him she didn't feel right about being with a married man. To make a long story short, the guy ended up leaving his wife. That's what he thought she really wanted. It was very sad. He lost his wife and his job over it.

Did she ever tell him the truth?

No, she told him that she just couldn't live with the guilt of breaking up his family. She lied in an effort to protect the man's feelings as well as his image of her. Over a year later when I talked to him, he was still trying to figure out what went wrong. He said he still loved her and believed she loved him. He thought there was a possibility that they would be together someday.

Okay. In that particular case, it would have been better to tell the guy he had a little dick. But, I am curious...why does the size of a man's penis matter so much?

You're kidding me, right?

No, I'm not kidding. Why does it matter?

When females are in their prime, they want to have intercourse. If a man has a small penis, a woman doesn't feel anything. It's just common sense. If you stick your finger into an empty mason jar you don't feel anything, do you? A larger penis stimulates the clitoris.

But if a woman doesn't screw around with every guy who comes along, she stays tight and doesn't have to worry about it.

No, Kevin. Then the *guy* doesn't have to worry about it. Men don't want to be judged like women for their physical attributes. Men don't want to be compared with other men like women have always been compared with other women. Do you know, when I was in junior high, my health teacher told our all-female class that we should wait to have sex until we were married because if we started having sex before then, we would be all used up and no man would want to marry us?

The myth that women get stretched out and used up if they sleep with a lot guys is just another one of the lies employed to deter females from having numerous sexual partners. Having a baby or passing a basketball through the vagina is going to stretch it out a bit, but a quarter-inch to an inch or two in circumference isn't going to make much of a difference.

Guys aren't worried that females will get stretched out from sleeping with other guys; they're afraid that females will find more enjoyable penises. Men are afraid that their penis is going to be compared to other penises.

So that's how women find out if guys have big penises. They mess around with them.

Sometimes they find out by word of mouth, through their girlfriends and through male friends of the men who have big penises.

Women don't mind if their friends sleep with the same guy they're sleeping with?

No, that's not how it works. Let's say a female meets a guy, has sex with him and then tells her friend, or friends, about the sexual encounter which includes the size of the guy's penis. One or more of the females she tells may at some future point seek out the guy and have sex with him, but she won't usually go back to her friends and talk about having done so.

It's kind of like when a guy gets a really good blow job. He tells his friends and then they try to get one, too.

It's a lot like that. I once interviewed a man who had been with several married women, nine to be exact. At the time that I interviewed him, I was already aware that females did this, so when he told me how many married women he had slept with, I knew he had to have a large penis. He also mentioned that he didn't go out looking for married women; they just seemed to find him. I remember thinking to myself at the time, *I'm sure they did.*

I ended up getting an interview with the married woman he was sleeping with at the time. I asked her if the guy was hung well and she said, very well. Then I asked her if, prior to sleeping with him, someone had told her about how big the guy's penis was. Her answer was yes, but she wondered how I knew. Turns out, one of her friends had slept with him a couple of years before, so she looked him up.

There was another guy I interviewed whose male friends regularly commented on the size of his penis. The majority of this guy's friends were married and, over the years, he'd slept with all but three of the eight wives. All of the wives had pursued him.

That blows my mind. I can't believe women do that. So, even if a woman is just naturally really tight, will she still want a guy who's hung pretty well?

This is really bugging you. I guess you must have a small penis.

It's not bugging me. I was just asking.

Kevin, even when a woman is really tight, when she gets really turned on—you know, really wet—her vagina opens up and even a large penis doesn't seem so large. However, a small penis can be frustrating and completely unfulfilling for a woman. I am telling you, this is just one more reason why men don't want to compete in the mating game. If men were aware of some of the desires that women have, they would have to compete the way women compete for men—hair, makeup, implants, clothes, you name it. Men would have to put a whole lot of work into competing for women just like women have for years ensured their support and survival by competing for men.

Men have always had to compete for women. They just compete with money.

But that leveled the playing field for all men, unattractive men and men with small penises.

You're right. Every guy knows, little dick or not, as long as he has cash he can get a woman.

Yeah, but what happens when women don't need money, when they have their own money, when they have the opportunity to provide for themselves? The problems we're facing today in our relationships are directly related to the fact that women are now in a position to provide for themselves. Many women no longer fear for their survival or financial support.

When a woman doesn't have to worry about herself financially, she's a lot more interested in physical appearance and sexual pleasure. We are just starting to see glimpses of women's natural sexual behavior. Our relationships are changing due to the opportunities that women now have.

Don't you think that's just a little extreme?

I don't think you realize how recently some of the changes in our society have occurred. For example, did you know that until the mid-seventies, most states didn't consider it a crime if a man raped his wife? I don't think it became a crime in New Jersey and Massachusetts until 1981.[2] Remember the women in Stage 1, the women who said sex for them was like a job? Up until recently, that's exactly what sex was for women—a job.

But it's not like that anymore. I still think you're being a little extreme.

Kevin, the changes have been very recent. Our belief systems haven't caught up yet. You and your wife were raised by parents who lived in a very different world. Hell, your grandma was raised right around the time women got the right to vote. Getting the vote was just the beginning; it wasn't until the women's movement in the sixties that we started seeing societal changes that would eventually enable women to make choices. Your beliefs about males and females reflect those of your parents. I think some people in government would say that our relationships are changing due to the growing independence of women.

A few years ago, on Christmas Eve morning while I was getting things ready for the holiday, I heard something on "Meet The Press" that caught my attention. Unfortunately I missed most of what was being discussed, so I sent for the transcripts.

Tim Russert asked the question, "Can government take steps to change people's value structure, to change the way they behave, to make them really want to have a family and understand the importance of that?"

And Newt Gingrich replied, "...There is the problem of modernity. I mean, Madonna having a child outside of marriage with her trainer...is in part, a reflection of the emerging independence of women and the fact that in a very wealthy society, you can choose many different styles of behavior..."

Russert said, "Can government have an impact? And what can George W. Bush do as our new president?"

Norton answered, "Well, you know, I certainly believe government can, faith-based institutions can, have an impact. I mean, I'm for having an impact in any way we can. For example, I'm for making marriage, which is going out of style—shame on Madonna—fashionable again. You know, I'm glad to see these things on television with people in wedding gowns and so forth. (Do) the media really want to be helpful? Try glamorizing marriage."

Some people may think that romanticism is the answer to some of the problems we are facing today, but by continuing to create a distorted image of marriage, we are only exacerbating our problems.

I'm not getting it. Why would the government want the media to glamorize or romanticize marriage?

In our country, romanticizing marriage might just be the only incentive left to encourage wealthy, educated people to get married. It's just like Newt Gingrich said, in a very wealthy society, you can choose many different lifestyles. Unless people believe that they want to get married, some will choose not to. Apparently from those transcripts, there are people in government who would rather that not happen.

Why though? I don't get it. What difference does it make if people don't get married? Who cares?

I don't know. Possibly it's because the more people think the same and the more rigid their beliefs, the easier they are to control and manipulate. So conformity could be one reason, but another reason could be money. Weddings are a multi-billion dollar industry. And divorce isn't exactly bad for the economy either.

When our past and present political figures preach about the importance of the family or family values, I think what they are really trying to do is condition people to believe that there is only one way to live—married with kids. Many people wind up assuming that marriage is a natural progression and fidelity a natural state. Do not choose marriage, assume marriage. Do not choose to have kids, assume kids. Do not choose fidelity, assume fidelity.

I don't know how anyone can think that distorting the truth about relationships will help. Getting married and having kids isn't right for everyone. Eventually we are going to have to acknowledge that reality or we will continue to see men and women inflicting pain on each other as well as their kids while attempting to come to terms with living a life they either don't want or are ill-prepared for. As it stands now, a lot of people don't really make conscious decisions about whether or not they want to be married until *after* they have gotten married, which I think is particularly true when it comes to women.

All women want is to get married. Every woman I have ever met wanted to get married.

That's what most women *think* they want. Women have always been taught that marriage is the goal of the human female.

That's why you can't make women happy, because they don't know what the hell they want.

You just hit the nail on the head. Women don't *know* what they want because they have not been allowed to *do* what they want until recently. You heard those transcripts from the Dr. Phil show. Attempts are still being made in this country to control girls' and women's sexual behavior. Continuing to shame females as well as trying to keep them ignorant about their sexuality isn't going to fix our problems. Our beliefs about female sexuality are nothing more than control systems in disguise. These beliefs are backfiring. They are bringing about the very thing they were intended to prevent.

As a matter of fact, have you seen anything lately on TV about women and their loss of sexual desire?

No, but I know Tracey has. One night she told me that it was normal for her not to want to have sex with me because

she heard something on TV about how millions of women don't want to have sex.

The problem isn't that women don't want to have sex, the problem is that women don't want to have sex with their husbands, which is very similar to the widespread problem we have been hearing about for years: men not wanting to have sex with their wives. Many married women have lost their primary motivation—fear. Like I said before, up until recently, sex was a married woman's job. Many women were afraid to decline their husbands sexually because to do so could jeopardize their financial security. Women felt as though they had to fight to keep their husbands. The media reinforced this belief. Books, articles, television, movies—advice on how to hold onto a husband was everywhere. Give him sex whenever he wants it, always wear make-up, don't make him wait for dinner, fuck him at the door! Women were inundated with advice on how to keep their husbands, and it was pretty much just accepted that men couldn't be faithful to them. Women also had to live with the constant fear of being traded in for a younger model. It has been ingrained into women's heads that men like younger women; being left for a younger woman is a fear that many women have to this day.

Don't you think you are exaggerating just a bit? I don't think it was really that bad.

No, I'm not exaggerating. It really was that bad. Not only would you be surprised, you would be amused by the advice that was given to women about how to please and keep a man. Thirty to thirty-five years ago, books such as *The Total Woman* and *The Sensuous Women* were bestsellers.

You can open either of these books to any page and get an idea of the fear women had and the lengths to which they would go to hang on to their husbands. Here, go ahead open the *The Sensuous Woman* any place you want and start reading.

"Nearly all men are polygamous by nature. Yet they face the terrible frustration of living in a monogamous society...left to themselves most men would probably never marry...it is natural for a man to have a wandering eye and a fertile imagination...he's not betraying you when he looks longingly at that

shapely blonde in the drugstore and dreams of devouring her. It's a natural instinct on his part and has nothing to do with the fact that he loves you very much. Married or not, men are going to continue looking and a great number will sample women besides yourself. You may not like it, but you're going to have to live with it. But it's women who keep marriage alive and benefit most from it. So get this straight. *If she is going to keep her man monogamous, it's the woman's responsibility to give him the sexual variety and adventure at home that he could find easily on his own elsewhere.* I know that's a tall order. You have to fight woman's most deadly sexual enemy—familiarity—for it breeds boredom in the male."[3]

Damn, you weren't kidding.

Unfortunately, our beliefs today are quite similar. Have you ever heard anyone, anywhere, talk about how familiarity breeds boredom in the female? Aren't most people still under the impression that women are naturally more monogamous than men? More monogamous does not mean monogamous. If you were inclined to have sex with a hundred women in your lifetime and I was inclined to have sex with thirty men, how could anyone think that I was more monogamous than you? The truth is, neither one of us would be monogamous. However, I've been using the word monogamous to mean sexually exclusive, since that is how most people interpret the word's meaning; however, monogamy is a particular form of marriage. The word does not mean sexually exclusive to one partner. It means being married to only one partner at a time.

Most people believe females prefer monogamy, but in *The Anatomy of Love*, Helen Fisher writes, "From a feminine perspective, pair-bonding is not normally adaptive either; a male can be more trouble than he is worth. Females of many species prefer to live with female relatives and copulate with visitors...A host of ecological and biological conditions must be present in the right proportions before perquisites exceed expenses, making monogamy the best—or only—alternative for both males and females of a species."[4]

Secrecy plays an important role in women's sexuality because of the reaction they fear from males. Though they appear to be more monogamous, they are just as likely as males to be unfaithful.

I find it interesting that the articles and TV specials I have seen on women's loss of sexual desire never mention that for the first time in history women can actually decline their husbands sexually without fear of financial or physical reprisals. I have never heard anyone mention that sex was a married woman's job or that just a few decades ago having sex for women wasn't contingent upon desire. The features I've seen all implied that women's disinterest in having sex with their husbands is a new phenomenon.

In fact, we have no way of knowing the true sexual appetite of women because we devalue women so much for having numerous sexual partners. Nor men's, for that matter, since we value men for the exact opposite—numerous sexual partners.

I think we know about men's sexual appetite. We want to have sex with as many women as we can.

Because it inflates your ego and makes you feel manly. Men not only gain self-esteem by having numerous sexual partners, they also gain self-esteem from believing and saying they want numerous sexual partners. It makes them feel good about themselves and superior to females.

I don't know about that, but I'm telling you, men are dogs. We want to have sex with everybody.

Have you ever declined sex with a female?

I have.

So I guess men won't sleep with just anybody.

Well, almost anybody.

Boys and men are particularly inclined to want sex with females who act like they don't want to have sex. Males like to believe sex is *for* them. They want to believe that any pleasure experienced by the female is *due to* them, due to their sexual abilities. I could walk up to a man today and tell him I wanted to have sex and I bet you a hundred dollars he would act like a scared school girl.

I disagree. If you did that, you would be getting laid, trust me.

Kevin, I experimented with this a couple times. On two occasions, I came flat out and said to a man, "I am not interested in anything other than sex. If you're looking for someone to go bowling with, it isn't me."

No, you didn't.

Yes, I did it, and just as I suspected, when I told those men that all I wanted from them was sex, they took on the role of the stereotypical female. Males, just like females, don't want to be *used* for sex. It makes both of the sexes feel worthless. Women in their prime quickly come to the realization that in order to have sex, initially they may have to pretend to be reluctant or, at the very least, sit back and wait for the man to initiate. A few women even told me they tried getting guys drunk in order to have sex with them.

Yeah, but what did the women look like?

That remark only confirms that males won't sleep with just anyone, but in any case, the women I'm referring to were attractive. One of them was *extremely* attractive. A guy actually told me that getting laid almost wasn't fun anymore because he said, "Nowadays, it just isn't that hard to get women to have sex with you."

Each sex believes that the other sex wants something entirely different, which continues to create an inordinate amount of desire in both of the sexes. It's what keeps the game going.

Much of men's power has been derived from erroneous beliefs about women, but the only way for these illusions to have become realities was for women to believe these things about themselves, too. Just look at other countries to see how the law became a legend. Do you think the women who are covered from head to toe hiding every part of their bodies to keep from being punished are naturally monogamous, or do you think they'd better be if they want to keep from being beaten or killed?

In many cases marriage and fidelity have been imposed on females through laws and customs. Because of these laws and customs, over time people have come to believe that women *want* to be married and that they are naturally monogamous.

Most people probably aren't even aware that it is women,

not men, who are most likely to leave their marriages. Yet we still perpetuate these erroneous beliefs.

Our society's false beliefs about women, combined with our beliefs in regard to men, specifically that men are dogs who don't want to get married, are causing lots of problems.

The authors of *Divorced Dads* say, …"Women are overwhelmingly the initiators in divorce…among all the studies that have examined the issue…" They also say, "…Few policymakers in the divorce arena know or even suspect the finding. The reason is that the result has not been well publicized…perhaps because of how politically unacceptable it is. To acknowledge the result suggests that men may not be entirely to blame for divorce, and that women are perhaps not so helpless and victimized as was thought. I call the fact that women overwhelmingly initiate modern divorces the 'dirty little secret' of divorce research."[5]

Women need to enter their marriages with the same knowledge about their sexuality that men have, or they're going to continue to make lifelong commitments based on illusions and moments of desire only to later break those commitments for the very same reasons.

I've got to get going, but I want to talk to you about this some more. I was serious when I said I wanted you to tell me everything you know about this.

I know you were.

Before I go I want to ask you something. Is there any way for me to know for sure if Tracey is seeing someone?

You mean aside from catching her cheating, or her admitting it?

Yes. I want to know if there are some sure-fire signs.

Well, "I'm not happy and I think we should separate," is a pretty good sign that someone else is in the picture.

Is there anything else?

Shaving is a pretty good indicator. Women who are having affairs typically start grooming and shaving their pubic area.

They also begin shaving their legs more thoroughly and regularly than they did previously. This is one of the reasons women become so guarded with their bodies when they are having affairs. It's not only because they are disinterested in having sex with their husbands. It's also because they don't want their husbands to notice the changes in their grooming habits.

Thanks...I'll get in touch with you soon.

July 2, 2003

I was surprised by Kevin's reaction to some of the things we talked about today. Kevin is not just well educated, he's street smart. And yet he struck me as rather naïve today. Then again, back when I first started researching this subject, he didn't have much interest in it. I remember joking with him about his disinterest in my new project. I said, "You know, Tracey's going to be thirty in a few years. You might want to look into some of this stuff." He answered, "I don't need to, I married a good woman." I recall thinking that if that was what he really believed, he was being stupid.

But it seems that that's what most men believe about their wives. If Kevin were listening to another man tell the same story he's telling he would immediately suspect that another guy was involved. Kevin, just like all the other men I've talked to, believes that cheating is something his wife would never do. What's interesting is that although females never give males any indication that they are anything less than 100 percent faithful, females seem to think males are stupid for believing them. Females just think males should know that when they say, "I would never cheat on you," what they really mean is, "I would never cheat on you as long as you don't piss me off too bad or as long as you don't piss me off too many times and as long as you make me happy and I don't get bored." Females think males should just know this about them—it should be a given.

Chapter 3

The Loss of Sexual Desire in Women

Did you mention any of the things we discussed to Tracey?

No. I'm not bringing anything up to Tracey until I have more information. In particular, I want to know more about women not wanting to have sex with their husbands. You said that in the past women had sex with their husbands in order to hang on to them, but that women don't have that incentive anymore. I would never leave Tracey and she hardly ever has sex with me.

Women still feel compelled to have sex with their husbands. Even though we don't insist that it's a woman's duty anymore, many girls are still taught while growing up that the only thing boys want from them is sex. You have no idea how many times a female may hear in her lifetime, "He doesn't really like you, he just wants to have sex with you." Whether from friends, family members, or the media, an impression is formed in the minds of females that, to a male they are only good for one thing. So, even after a woman gets married, she continues to feel an underlying pressure to satisfy her husband sexually in order to keep him. Books are still written on how to get, or keep, a man. Yet women leave men the majority of the time.

But how much of that has to do with men being assholes?

Do you think you're an asshole?

No, I don't think I'm an asshole, but I think a lot of men are.

Surprisingly, many women told me that their husbands were great guys. Many just thought their husbands were boring.

If you haven't seen the movie, "Unfaithful," you should rent it. It's about a happily married woman who has an affair. With the exception of the ending, it's pretty true to form. And remember, in the information I sent you the women in Stage 1 were happy. They loved their lives. The only problem they had was a disinterest in sex. I stayed in contact with a few of the women I originally interviewed. The very same women who loved their husbands and their lives eventually moved through the other stages.

Because men and women are so uncomfortable talking about this, it becomes a major area of contention in many marriages. It's interesting that the majority of the men I have talked to feel the same way you do. It's not the sex they miss so much; it's their wives' affection.

That's exactly what I miss. She won't even touch me and she won't let me touch her, either.

I know. She's afraid you'll want to have sex, so she avoids you. I told you the first time we talked that this was complicated. There are several reasons why women feel the way they do today. Don't make the mistake of concluding that any one thing I tell you is causing the problem. It's a combination of many things.

Having said that, I don't think men are aware that sex for women is a lot of work. I don't think men have any idea how much preparation women put into having sex. The decision to have sex with a man is usually not spur of the moment. Decisions are made prior to dates because of all the prep work involved. In fact, I bet you could paint your living room and kitchen in less time than it takes for some women to get ready to have sex.

It can't take that long. What the hell do they have to do?

I'm telling you it can take up to eight hours for women to prepare for sex. Suppose a woman meets a man she's attracted to and decides to have sex with him. The first thing she will probably do is go shopping for a new bra and underwear. Including drive time, that takes an hour and a half, minimum. The next thing she will probably do is either go somewhere to get a manicure and pedicure or give them to herself. Easy two hours, because she can't do anything until her nails are dry. After that, she has to take a shower, which can take up to thirty minutes, because she has to shave her legs, underarms and, nowadays, even her pubic hair.

After a woman takes her shower and shaves, she has to put on makeup and do her hair. Depending on the woman that could take one to two hours. Then she may spend thirty to forty-five minutes trying to figure out what to wear. So just to prepare to have sex, this woman has already invested roughly four to five hours. However, this does not include the time she will need to clean her house if she is planning on having sex there, or if, heaven forbid, she has to cook the man dinner.

I'm telling you, it can be a lot of work for women to have sex. Actually, it can be a real pain in the ass. This should shed some light on why women get so upset when men change or cancel plans at the last minute. Often they are not nearly as upset about not seeing the guys as they are about having spent so much time and effort in preparation. Imagine how men would feel if they had to pay for their dates with women in advance. A change in plans would result in wasted cash—much like the wasted time and energy cancelled plans represent for females.

I hear what you're saying, but women don't do all that stuff after you marry them. I know, I've been married twice and neither one of my wives did any of that stuff after we got married.

How could they? Both of your wives had kids and jobs. How could they have spent eight hours a day preparing to have sex, or even two or three hours for that matter?

I'm just saying that once a woman gets married, she stops doing all that stuff. So why wouldn't she feel like having sex then? It's not as big of a pain in the ass as it was before.

Because women associate the *preparations* for sex, with the *desire* to have sex, kind of like guys associate football with beer. Most women don't consider themselves attractive enough to feel sexual without the props—you know, the hair and makeup, all that stuff. Going through the process creates excitement and anticipation. It's almost like foreplay, but there is no way a woman can do all that stuff on a daily basis—at least without it becoming like a job.

Eventually, women begin to associate sex with work. That's how the brain operates. We associate certain things with certain other things. When you bought your first house, for example, you probably went out and purchased a new lawn mower. You probably couldn't wait to mow the lawn. But let's face it, after awhile you began to associate the lawn mower with work. It's the same thing with women and sex.

Our society's standards of female beauty have gotten so far away from the way women look naturally that when women look anything close to natural, they feel unattractive and completely non-sexual.

Men don't really care about that stuff, though, its women that care about it. I wouldn't care if Tracey didn't wear makeup or shave.

Some men don't care about that stuff, just like some women don't care about it.

Here's my point: Overall, society promotes the notion that women want to get married and men just want to screw around. So to get what they *think* they want from men, women assume a lot of work is required. These beliefs have developed into an exciting and challenging game for women—trying to get men to fall in love with, or marry, them. Striving for something or looking forward to it causes a stimulant effect in the brain.

That really pisses me off. I mean, it's crazy. Women are screwed up.

Is it any more screwed up than the game men play with women— the I'm-only-interested-in-you-until-you-have-sex-with-me game? You know damn well that you and almost every other man play that game repeatedly. Remember, men acquired much of their sexual and relationship power by creating societies in which females needed them for survival. In the past, marriage served important purposes for both sexes, but it was particularly beneficial, if not crucial, to the survival and financial support of women. Today it's the opposite. Because of the opportunities available to women today, more and more are beginning to believe that marriage is more beneficial to men.

People in government preaching about family values while the media romanticizes marriage only makes things worse. Romanticism may make women want to marry, but it also causes them to leave their husbands. Since it is believed that women want to be married and that they aren't naturally inclined to screw around, any unhappiness or infidelity on the part of women is assumed to be due to the men they married.

Women today are encouraged to find men who are sensitive and faithful and many are succeeding. The problem is, once a woman realizes that she has found and attained what she was looking for she may become bored as shit. What the hell do you do after you have obtained everything you ever wanted? Compared to the importance of finding the right man and getting married, everything else in life pales by comparison.

For several years a new trend has been developing in male-female relationships. In the past, men had the upper hand in marriage. Today the opposite is true. More and more women are recognizing that they, in fact, have the upper hand in marriage, and many of them are abusing that power just as many men abuse theirs.

Unfortunately, what's happening today has little to do with balance or equality. Many women are either knowingly or unknowingly taking on the past roles of men.

The more we talk, the angrier I get.

If you get mad, you won't be able to understand what I'm telling you. The information wouldn't make you so angry if you didn't see the similarities between the game you played when you were younger—pursuing and discarding females—and the game that females play today. The feeling a woman has after she gets a man to fall in love with her isn't any different from the feeling you had after convincing a girl or woman to have sex with you. Didn't you think it was fun to see if you could get a female into bed?

You know, I did. But all guys do.

You do realize that you and other males wouldn't be able to have fun at our expense if it weren't for the belief that "some girls do" and "some girls don't," right? If females everywhere stood up and said, "Guess what? We all do," the sex game would be over. Males would have to seek their excitement in another way, just as women will eventually have to seek excitement in some way other than trying to get men to commit to them.

At some point, people grow up. Tracey and I are adults with kids and responsibilities. We're not teenagers.

Tracey may be an adult, but she's also a woman in her thirties whose body is receiving subconscious signals from testosterone. Those signals are triggering feelings she may not understand. We don't teach women about them. It's easier to be responsible when you are informed, don't you think? Why do you think Tracey will handle this phase of her life any differently than you handled the corresponding phase in yours?

Because she's an adult. We've got two kids. She can't just run off and start screwing around.

Why? You did.

I was a *kid*!

No, you weren't. You were a twenty-six year old man with a child and responsibilities. You need to understand that what you felt back then is pretty similar to what Tracey is probably feeling right now. The difference is you *knew* you liked to screw around. You *knew* the feelings you had were natural. But it doesn't occur to you that familiarity might have the same effect on Tracey.

Over time, many females lose their desire to have sex with the same partner. That is when they usually *change* partners. I'll give you an example. Remember when we were younger, back when your brother was dating Lisa? Why do you think your brother's girlfriend told him that she just wanted to be friends? She was saying, in effect, "I don't want to have sex with *you* anymore, I want to have sex with somebody else."

I think she thought he was screwing around on her. And every once in awhile he probably was.

That's probably what your brother thought, too. You have no idea how guilty Lisa felt for ending their relationship. But she wanted to be with another guy. Your brother would have liked to continue seeing Lisa, while occasionally screwing around on the side. Lisa, on the other hand, thought of herself as a good girl, so when she no longer got high from being with your brother and became attracted to Doug, she dumped your brother. In her mind, your brother was the right guy until Doug came along and then Doug was the right guy.

I see women do that all the time. Women are always trying to trade up!

No, they don't always trade *up*—they trade *different*. Women are just as likely to trade down. It's how they fulfill their desire for sexual variety. Because of our beliefs, males are more likely to cheat and females are more likely to turn partners. After a while in a relationship, it's natural for sexual desire to wane. Otherwise there wouldn't be so many books out there trying to tell us how to keep the sex alive after we're married. You never hear about books on how to keep your appetite alive *after* you get married, do you? Whether you're with the right one or the wrong one, long-term fidelity is not natural.

The chemicals released in our bodies as a result of frequent and regular contact with our sexual partners are similar to the chemicals released to solidify attachment bonds, including the attachment bonds we develop with our children and siblings. This is why over time, many people feel their spouse is like a brother or sister, or a mother or father, instead of a sexual partner.

Grab the *The Chemistry of Love*. It's behind you on the second shelf. Read the first page that's book-marked.

Okay, it says: "Biologically, it appears that we have evolved two distinct chemical systems for romance; one basically serves to bring people together. The first is attraction. Attraction is the excitement we feel when falling in love, and is quite similar to what happens when we take a stimulant drug. The second, which helps keep people together, is attachment. Attachment has more to do with feelings of security than of excitement. It too has a number of drug analogies, although surprisingly it may have more to do with narcotics than any other drug type."[1]

Helen Fisher theorizes that humans originally evolved a four-year breeding cycle. If this is true, then the feelings we experience in our romantic relationships are in sync with our breeding cycle.[2]

In *Mean Genes*, the authors state, "Our divorce patterns also reflect sexual issues. Contrary to the popular notion of a seven-year-itch, people are most likely to divorce in the fourth year of marriage. This four-year-itch is scratched across more than sixty radically different cultures."[3]

With these things in mind, one could speculate that continuing a sexually exclusive relationship with the same partner for more than four years is unnatural. In *The Myth of Monogamy*, the authors point out, "...Among most monogamous mammals, sexual behavior is neither especially frequent nor especially fervent. ...In most species, when the pair-bond is well established, relatively little energy is expended on sex..."[4]

This would explain the disinterest in sex that many women today are experiencing and it would also explain why you lost interest in Jill, your first wife.

Yes, it would. I wasn't interested in having sex with Jill because of that brother-sister feeling. I really loved Jill, but I just couldn't get past the sex thing.

So, you did what a lot of people do. You had an affair. If people weren't so afraid to talk about this, it wouldn't end up being such a big problem.

But, you're saying its natural, which I guess means there isn't anything we can do about it.

As a culture we need to stop pretending that the drive to mate with different partners will not exist if we are with the "right" person.

Our instinctual drives can only run our lives because we are denying that they exist. Denying and being ashamed of our animal nature causes a lot of problems. People can't choose their behavior if they are trying to deny that certain behaviors exist, particularly if the behavior involves reproduction—the driving force motivating every living thing.

When you say it like that it sounds as if there really *isn't* anything people can do.

Remember, we have the ability to manipulate our brain chemistry through our behavior. However, most people aren't aware of this, and many relationships inevitably wind up going from attraction to attachment to screwing around and/or breaking up.

So, what can you do, once a woman stops wanting to have sex? Can you change it?

Touching can make a big difference because it increases oxytoxin levels, which in turn increase sexual receptivity.[5] However, the touching needs to be non-sexual in nature.

When women start getting that uncomfortable feeling about sleeping with their husbands and they start making excuses not to have sex, they're usually scared. The feeling is familiar to them. They've experienced it before in prior relationships. They are also afraid of their husband's reaction to their disinterest in sex. They're afraid their husband will cheat on them or eventually leave them because of it. It's like having a problem falling asleep when you know that you have to get up early. Your fear of not being able to sleep actually keeps you awake. Women's fear of not wanting to have sex keeps them from ever wanting sex. They become preoccupied with their disinterest in sex. Men may even fuel their wife's fear by implying that they may go elsewhere for sex or leave them because of it, which is the worst thing a man can do if he wants to help the situation.

You said what you missed most was your wife's affection. You also said you wouldn't leave Tracey just because she wouldn't have sex with you, right?

Yes.

In the beginning, did you lead her to believe that you might?

I don't know. I definitely let her know that I wasn't happy about it.

Would *you* want to have sex with someone who was threatening to betray you?

Men don't know what to do. They're afraid they might have to live their whole life without sex.

It's not about sex, it's about the ego. Whether it's the man who loses sexual desire, or the woman, it creates ego problems for the spouse. The desire to have sex becomes obsessive to the one, while the desire not to have sex becomes obsessive to the other. Eventually, these feelings and behaviors become habitual in the relationship.

After the natural feelings of mating dissipate, many couples go on automatic, disconnecting from each other even further. Eventually either the relationship ends or the partners stay in the relationship and seek emotional and sexual connections elsewhere.

However, if a couple can communicate and alleviate sexual pressure while maintaining the affection in their relationship, there's a possibility they can begin what I call the "pass-through effect." That's when a couple moves their relationship to a level beyond animal mating. And before you start telling me about how much you love Tracey, I want you to remember that the feelings of attachment you have for her are also a part of the mating process.

What's that supposed to mean?

It means that many relationships serve the same purpose as a security blanket does to a child. Eventually, children realize that their blanket gives them nothing, which is the same realization people often experience regarding their relationships

I don't think that's the case with me and Tracey.

I hope not. But Kevin, truly connected couples don't have to guess how their partners feel. If you're spending *any* of your time *wondering* about what Tracey is thinking and feeling, then something is wrong.

In many marriages, spouses pay very little attention to each other at all. Women especially seem to make this complaint about their husbands.

However, women often treat their husbands like a piece of furniture sitting in the middle of the room that they have to avoid bumping into. Basically, they make their husbands feel like they're a nuisance.

Tracey didn't used to treat me that way, but she does now.

You said something about eliminating sexual pressure, how do you do that?

Most women I talked to who'd lost sexual desire said they felt as though their husbands wanted to have sex all the time. Even if their husbands only approached them about sex once a week, they felt sexual pressure on a daily basis. It can be helpful for couples to negotiate and come to an agreement on the frequency of sex as opposed to waiting until both partners feel the desire.

But who wants that? What about spontaneity? It doesn't sound like it would be worth it.

If that's the way you feel then you just proved my point. It's not about sex, because if it were, you wouldn't mind sacrificing spontaneity in order to get laid.

I'm just saying that planning the date and time you're going to have sex would take a lot of the enjoyment out of it.

I set up an appointment each week to get a massage. Not only do I enjoy it, I also look forward to it. It can be the same with sex, even for couples that have been together for a long time.

I still don't like the idea of having to set up an appointment to have sex with my own wife!

I'm going to say it again—this isn't about sex. Tracey's not wanting to have sex with you is affecting your ego. What you really want is for her to *desire* you. If you think about this, you'll realize that when avoidance of sex began to occur in your marriage you were bothered by the possibility that Tracey could have feelings similar to your own. Tracey's resistance is causing you to feel insecure and you're hiding your insecurity with anger, which pushes her away even further. She probably feels as though having sex with you is her job. And besides, who wants to have sex with someone who's *mad* at them? Tracey more than likely feels hurt by your lack of understanding. But, like you, instead of expressing her pain, she's expressing anger.

People like to pretend that their spouses don't have the same feelings that they have. Our egos can't bear the thought of our spouse wanting someone else. Men are likely to convince themselves that their wives don't like sex. It's easier than acknowledging that their wives might have desires similar to their own.

I think that on some level men know that women are attracted to other men, but women don't admit having such thoughts. If I asked my wife or any other woman if she thinks about screwing around, she would say, "No, I never even think about it."

Females are programmed to say that, but remember, the programming is intended to ease the male's insecurity about paternity. Females know they can lose value for admitting such thoughts.

Finish what you were saying about getting rid of sexual pressure.

Designating a specific time to have sex, or a general frequency, takes away the daily feeling of sexual pressure. Women don't feel as though they need to be cold and unaffectionate towards their husbands, because they know that their affection isn't going to be misinterpreted as a sexual gesture.

If couples make such an arrangement, however, it's important that both people adhere to the agreement. In other words, there shouldn't be any pushing for more sex than what is agreed upon, and it's crucial for couples to continue touching. Not only can non-sexual affection bring back sexual desire, it is also important to our health. People can get sick from not being touched. People can actually die from lack of human contact.[6]

In other words, Tracey's killing me.

It's nice to know you haven't lost your sense of humor.

I'm curious about something. Why don't I have that brother/sister feeling for Tracey. Why do I still want to have sex with her?

Kevin, you said that Tracey's disinterest in having sex with you has been going on for a long time. According to her, she is not happy and wants to separate. You know that saying, "Fear is a great motivator." You're scared, and because of your fear, you're powerfully motivated to hold on to Tracey or win her back.

Tracey is my wife. I love her. This isn't about trying to win her back. It's not some game I'm playing. This is about my wife and kids!

Kevin, I know you don't want to believe that your passion for Tracey is intensified by her disinterest, but it is. Let me remind you of something. Do you remember about two years ago, when we went to lunch with your brother?

Yeah, I remember.

Do you remember what we talked about that day?

I'm sure we talked about a lot of things.

Remember the waitress—the one you and your brother couldn't take your eyes off?

Don't even go there. I didn't do anything. You know I wouldn't even think about cheating on Tracey.

That's where you and most people are completely full of shit. Of course you think about it.

It's our inability to acknowledge our natural sexual impulses that causes so many of us to wind up being controlled by them. Fear creates the problems. We try to avoid our sexual energy, and it's impossible. Most sexual urges would be fleeting if we didn't consider them taboo. Guilt and denial are what cause urgings to become fixations.

For years, you and I have had conversations about this. You have told me time and again that men would prefer to be married while having sex with other women on the side. When I interview men, I always ask them about this and their eyes light up. They think it sounds like a great idea until I mention that their wives would get to screw around, too. Then they don't seem to like the idea very much.

Listen, I have no desire to sleep with anyone else.

Right now you don't, but if you felt one-hundred percent secure in your relationship, like you did two years ago, you'd be whistling a different tune. Faithfulness gives men a sense of accomplishment, because it goes against their nature. Due to conditioning, women feel just the opposite. *Trying* to be faithful doesn't seem natural to them.

Let's be honest, Kevin, you've been patting yourself on the back for years for remaining faithful. Your self-satisfaction would be much less if you didn't feel you were accomplishing a tremendous feat. You feel so guilty about what you did to Jill in your first marriage that you are trying to make up for it in the second. It's a common scenario for men in second marriages, as well as for men who marry late and men who are trying to be better husbands than their fathers were. Men enter marriage with repressed feelings of guilt, while women enter marriage with repressed feelings of anger.

I do feel bad about being unfaithful to my first wife. That's why I promised myself never to do anything like that again.

But Tracey, like a lot of women, may not have made a similar commitment. Instead, she may have just made an assumption—the assumption that she would never *desire* to be with somebody else. A conscious decision is very different from an assumption. Why commit to avoiding something you'll never want to do? Like I said, *trying* to be faithful doesn't seem natural to women.

Basically females are faithful as long as they don't feel the urge to be unfaithful, is that what you're saying?

No, I'm saying that females aren't as comfortable with their sexual urges as men are, particularly when they are in a relationship. In order to maintain the fantasy that females are naturally monogamous, society has always denied that females have powerful sexual urges. So having them doesn't seem as natural to women as it does to men.

I want to let some of this sink in. I'll get in touch with you after I've had some time to think.

July 9, 2003

Today, Kevin wanted advice on how to rekindle sexual desire. I think he's under the impression that if he does what I recommend he will be able to fix his problems with Tracey. Unfortunately, if someone else has entered the picture it's probably too late for that. Tracey's problem will no longer be rooted in a loss of sexual desire, but in the awakening of sexual desire. If her experiences are like those of other women I've interviewed, she is consumed with thoughts of sex. However, her sexual thoughts and fantasies probably don't include Kevin. It's interesting that Kevin understood immediately what I was talking about during our first conversation, when I explained that Tracey was probably experiencing the brother-sister feeling that develops in long-term relationships. However, like most men, he gets it and then forgets it. You can't fix the problems in Stage 3 with the remedies for Stage 1.

Chapter 4

The Commitment Game: Female Version of Pursue and Discard

It's been awhile. Are things better between you and Tracey?

No. Everything is exactly the same.

Have you tried talking to her?

I've tried, but she refuses to talk about it.

Have you asked her if she's met someone?

Yes, I did. She said no, and that was the end of the conversation.

Are you saying that she responded in a way that shut down the conversation?

Pretty much.

Did you believe she was telling you the truth?

I don't know what to believe anymore. I just know that I've got to make this work. I don't want to lose my kids.

When you called yesterday, you said you had some questions for me. What do you want to talk about?

During one of our conversations, you said that a lot of women enter their marriages with suppressed anger. Why?

What are they so angry about? Is it the way guys have treated them in the past? Is that what it is?

Yes, women are angry in part because they've grown up under a double standard, but also because of circumstances they've put up with in order to get married. When a woman wants to get married, she will usually overlook a lot, and at times allow herself to be treated pretty badly. After she gets married, not only is the excitement of pursuit over, after a few years of marriage the attraction buzz has dissipated, too. At that point, many women may find that marriage hasn't even come close to meeting their expectations. Some women feel stupid for having wanted it so badly in the first place, especially since marriage probably increased their workload.

What are women expecting when they get married?

They're expecting the feeling to last, the feeling they had while they were pursuing their lover and looking forward to fulfilling their fantasy.

I guess that's why women are always trying to change men. They don't necessarily want the guy—they just want to get married.

Yes, that's often the case. Females want to wear the dress and have the wedding. Women like the *idea* of getting married. Many women have looked forward to that day their whole lives, which ultimately sets them up for a huge crash.

Most women are happiest when focused on fulfilling some part of the get-married-and-live-happily-ever-after fantasy. They are content, even in relatively unfulfilling relationships, as long some part of the fantasy is left to play out.

First, women focus on getting the man, then they focus on planning the wedding, then they focus on being a good wife and buying and decorating a house, then they focus on having a baby and, finally, they focus on why they wanted all this in the first place.

Contrary to popular assumption, women don't put nearly as much effort into their relationships with their boyfriends and husbands as they put into trying to accomplish their goal of getting married and becoming a wife and mother. It's only *after* they've accomplished these goals that they begin to evaluate the relationship itself.

I guess that's why men have all the power before marriage and women have it after marriage. A woman will behave any way she thinks a man wants her to prior to marriage. She won't bitch about a thing. But after you marry her, you find out she doesn't like a fucking thing about you!

Do you know how bad it feels to have your wife look at you as though you're the single most disappointing thing in her life? But she'll never tell you why she's so disappointed, or how you can stop disappointing her. And what's really fucked up is, if you can't guess what she wants you don't get to live with your kids.

Do you know why men don't like to talk to their wives? It's because every conversation is a guessing game. Talking to a woman is like playing a game of chess. Men think that when they find a woman who really loves them, they'll be able to talk about some of the things that really bother them, or for that matter, the things that really matter to them. But it doesn't take men long to realize that life will be a lot more peaceful if they just keep their mouths shut. When a woman says, "Tell me how you feel," she really means, "Make me feel good!"

I know you're angry. I wish I could say you are wrong, but I agree with you. Women often petition for more intimacy in their relationships, but many of them have as much difficulty with intimacy as men.

Even though many women claim they want to be with men who are open and honest, because of their own problems with intimacy, they often form relationships with men who are emotionally inaccessible. Instead of choosing men who are interested in developing a relationship, these women choose men who make them feel insecure. Insecurity can create motivation and excitement. Women who seek excitement in their marriages (and many do) will often forego the possibility of real relationships for the excitement of fantasy relationships.

Women fall in love quickly, whereas men fall in love slowly, over a longer period of time. Women decide rather quickly—sometimes instantly—whether or not a man is "the guy." The men who are christened Mr. Right may not even know that they have been chosen.

When it comes to marriage, women are conditioned to believe that men are the "choosers," while they are the ones waiting to be chosen. This makes them more inclined to go after men who are unattainable or unavailable, so they can remain excited for an indefinite period of time. Females want the excitement to last, and for them it does last—until after they have a commitment. However, once they accomplish their goal, the feeling of excitement goes away, which is very disappointing because the excitement was what they wanted and they thought it would last.

It's not uncommon for women to pine for men who shy away from commitment, while they shun the attention given to them by men who are willing and ready to make a commitment. Males have similar feelings prior to having sex with females. If females were taught to believe that males wanted to get married, they wouldn't be challenged or excited about getting men to marry them.

Unfortunately for men, women tend to end their relationships in the same way they start them, without men ever being the wiser. A man may not be aware that a woman has chosen him to be "Mr. Right," and he may be equally unaware when she decides he is no longer "Mr. Right." When a woman says that she is leaving a relationship, there is usually nothing the man can do to stop her, because she has already made her decision. She may give numerous reasons why she is leaving; however, she is not interested in working on the relationship. She already has another "Mr. Right" picked out or is eager to find one. She is looking for the feeling of excitement again.

You would think at our age relationships wouldn't be such a pain in the ass. I got married because I didn't want to play games anymore. I get so damn tired of hearing, "I'm not happy, I'm not happy." If Tracey doesn't know why she's not happy, how the hell can I know?

I hope that before long, people will begin to acknowledge what I call the "female crisis," which is similar to the male midlife crisis, only a lot worse. After a couple of years of researching this, I realized that what I experienced was textbook behavior, so to speak. I don't know if I ever told you, but in the beginning, when I first started having those "I'm not happy feelings" in my own marriage, I went to see a psychologist.

No, you never told me that.

On my first visit, I told the psychologist how I'd been feeling. I explained that I'd been happy for the first few years, but that for some reason no longer was. I told her I found myself extremely attracted to other men, and I specifically asked her if what I was feeling was normal.

What did she say?

She said my feelings could be due to needs that were not being met by my husband.

So, she said it was your husband's fault.

No, she said it *could* be my husband's fault.

However, much later, through my own research, I learned that what I was feeling was quite natural. In, *A Woman's Book of Life*, Joan Borysenko says, "The peak time of divorce for women is while they are in their late twenties and early thirties after an average of four years of marriage."[1]

Taking into consideration that the high we get from our partners may be all but gone after four years, and keeping in mind that women enter their sexual peak in their late twenties and early thirties, you can understand that just from a biological standpoint marital fidelity can actually be more difficult for women than it is for men. Men who marry in their mid-to-late twenties are moving away from their sexual prime, while women of the same age are just reaching theirs.

Women who marry in their mid-twenties can experience a biological double-whammy—hitting their sexual prime coupled with the natural waning of sexual desire for their partner. However, these are just the biological factors. From a psychological standpoint, many women also get hit twice—first by the letdown the occurs when marriage fails to meet their unrealistic expectations, and second by a fear of getting older, which many women experience as they approach thirty.

Not too long ago you couldn't find a fashion model over twenty-five. Women over that age weren't considered attractive enough to photograph. You would be shocked if you went back twenty-five or thirty years and looked at pictures of female celebrities in their thirties and compared them to celebrities in their thirties today. Years ago, at a certain age, women bowed out. They believed the men-look-better-with-age and women-just-look-like-shit mentality that existed until very recently in our culture.

When you take all these things into consideration, the late twenties and thirties can really be more like a quadruple-whammy for women. It's common knowledge that men can suffer from a midlife crisis in their forties. It should also be common knowledge that women can suffer a similar crisis, only possibly to a greater degree, in their late twenties and thirties.

Men should be prepared for this. Men should know about this prior to getting married.

Women *and* men should know about this prior to getting married. It's something both sexes should be aware of.

I don't understand why people don't talk about this. It just doesn't make sense.

Because it would require that we acknowledge the female sex drive, including the drive to mate with more than one partner. Women have always been *told* what they like sexually. Did you know Freud encouraged women to have orgasms through intercourse alone, without clitoral stimulation? I think possibly this misinformation persisted until the 1940s. Can you imagine somebody telling you that the only way you could have an orgasm was if someone stuck a finger in your ass?

My point is, we are still uncomfortable with the idea that women really like sex. The thought of females being naturally inclined to desire multiple sexual partners is something society isn't ready to acknowledge yet. But I don't see how we can solve our relationship problems by ignoring this fact.

Females like sex. Many of them don't know how much until they reach their prime. When women are in they're prime, they lose their inhibitions and they're not afraid to say what they want. However, they may be so used to the role they have taken on in their marriages that they don't feel comfortable sharing that part of themselves with their husbands.

What do women want sexually? Do they want to have sex as often as men do?

The biggest difference I have noticed between men and women is that women seem to prefer more sex per episode than men. For example, if a typical man wants to have sex three days a week, a typical woman is more likely to prefer weekly or twice weekly sex for two to three hours each time. That's why women in their prime like having sex with younger guys. It takes longer for women to become aroused and satisfied. Men in their thirties and up can have a more difficult time reaching orgasm more than once. Women may still be wanting more sex at that point. You know how men tend to want to go to sleep after they have an orgasm? Most women want to sleep when sexually satisfied, too.

Women need to be warmed up for sex with talking and affection, and they also may want to be talked to during sex. Talking and affection are necessary for females to achieve arousal and pleasure. Men need to understand that a woman's having sex without either of these components can be likened to a man's having sex without an erection.

Do women want men to talk dirty to them?

Before sex women typically like to connect with men through non-sexual touching and conversation. However, during sex some women want men to talk dirty to them, or at least to talk in sexual terms. Other women may just want to be told how much the man loves them and/or desires them. And, of course, for many women desires are contingent upon mood. It just depends on the woman, but one thing is for certain, once women experience the type of verbal stimulation they like, they usually find sex less fulfilling without it.

Really?

Yes, most of the women I talked to mentioned how much they liked some type of verbal stimulation during sex.

So, women like to have more than one orgasm every time they have sex.

Not necessarily every time, but for women in their prime, one orgasm may not be enough. Try to remember what you wanted sexually when you were in your teens and twenties.

It probably wasn't uncommon for you to be as horny after sex as you were before. And yet the female you were with, if she was the same age, probably wasn't interested. It's the same thing only in reverse. Men in their thirties and forties tend to be satisfied after having sex while women of the same age are just getting warmed up.

Women want talking, affection, foreplay, orgasm, and then more of the same. Males may want sex more often, but females seem to want more sex per sitting, which may be another reason why they think sex isn't that big a deal. They are rarely completely satisfied.

Intercourse alone can make a woman feel as though the man is using her to masturbate. It just doesn't do much for her. Even when there is foreplay, it isn't necessarily fulfilling, because some men aren't nearly as interested in pleasing their partner as they are in preparing her vagina for intercourse. A man will usually kiss a woman, touch her breasts and then reach between her legs to see if she's wet before jumping on top of her. And that's only the first couple of times. After that, it's hit and miss. The third or fourth time a female has sex with a guy, he's likely to skip the kiss, skip their breast, and jump on top.

Some men also have a tendency to treat a woman's vagina as a separate entity, as though her vagina isn't connected to her. When a man gropes and grabs at his wife's body it can make her feel disconnected from the experience. It may also trigger memories of past experiences where she felt used or violated.

But why don't women just say what they want?

Some women are not aware of what they like sexually. Those who do know may feel uncomfortable articulating what they want.

Why? Why would they feel uncomfortable saying what they want?

Females are passive when they're young—much more so than when they are older. They get used to letting males take the lead sexually. Many females also experience negative consequences when they are sexually aggressive. Remember the story you told me about the girl who gave you a blow job in high school? Your reaction wasn't unusual. Females learn to act passive and innocent even when they aren't. They don't say what they want because they're afraid they will be rejected if they do. They can't say what they want and appear innocent. And they don't wish to come across as hard to please. With younger men, women are much more comfortable being aggressive, and younger males don't mind taking direction. They tend to be eager to please older women. Perhaps they feel a bit intimidated by their experience. Younger men and older women don't usually play games with each other either. Both are interested in relationships where freedom, independence and orgasms are the top priorities.

It's interesting that all these women who seem to be completely disinterested in sex are actually hornier than they have ever been in their lives.

I know, I think the programs I used to watch on TV regarding this subject should have been titled, "Women Who *Seem to* Suffer from Loss of Sexual Desire."

Yes, they should have.

Interestingly, there was a point during my research when I suspected that familiarity affected females *more* than it affects males, not because of their disinterest in having sex with their husbands, but because they were so repulsed by the idea.

I've wondered at times if there might not be a biological basis for the aversion women have to marital sex. The majority of the women I talked to didn't have any interest in sex, unless it was with a new partner. The men I talked to, although they readily admitted their desire for different sexual partners, whether they were faithful to their wives or not still wanted to have sex with their wives, whereas the majority of the women preferred no sex at all over marital sex.

I found that females tended to like sex with new partners in the beginning of the relationship. It was almost as though a switch was flipped at some point in the relationship that shut off their sexuality. I stayed in contact with a few of the women I interviewed in Stage 1 (the loss of sexual desire stage) as they moved through the stages. While they were in Stage 1, they said things like, "The thought of having sex makes my skin crawl," or "Thinking about sex makes me sick to my stomach," or "I could go the rest of my life without ever having sex again." These same women were swinging from chandeliers when they found new partners.

It seems as though women temporarily shut down after they've been with the same partner for a period of time. Many go through a completely non-sexual period. They don't masturbate or think about sex at all and their disinterest in sex lasts until they find themselves attracted to someone else.

Even women who found sex irritating or painful with their husbands because of vaginal dryness were miraculously cured when a new partner entered the picture. As one woman put it, "It turns out, the desert has an oasis."

As I mentioned in our previous conversation, the women I talked with were often consumed with trying to find ways to get out of having sex. It became a fixation.

The stories of the women I talked with were incredibly similar. At some point in their intimate relationships, these females, whether young or old, turned off sexually. They desired sex in the beginning of relationships and they also loved affair sex. But they didn't like marital sex, or at minimum they could take it or leave it. Don't get me wrong, men love affair sex too, but the men I talked to said they also liked having sex with their wives. And men were much more likely to prefer intercourse to masturbation, while many of the women said just the opposite.

Really, women would rather masturbate than have sex with their husbands?

That's what a lot of the women said. However, keep in mind that when women allow men to bring them to orgasm, they risk not having one or taking forever to achieve it. If there's one false move or one slip of the tongue on the male's part, it's all over, no orgasm.

If women would tell men what they want, that wouldn't happen.

No, even then, the process is easily disrupted. For example, sometimes when a woman says, "That feels good," or "I'm coming," her partner tries to intensify the experience by doing something a little different rather than continuing exactly the same stimulation. When this happens, the intensity of the orgasm often diminishes or the woman ends up having no orgasm at all.

Women feel tremendous pressure to reach orgasm quickly. They think a man's willingness to give them pleasure is contingent upon achieving quick results, and that anything longer will hinder the man's sexual pleasure. When they masturbate, however, most women reach orgasm very quickly, unless they intentionally postpone it to make the experience last longer. So, the pressure not only lengthens the time required to achieve orgasm, it may inhibit orgasm. When it comes to orgasms, many women find masturbation to be just good time management.

Whether young or old, many women find sex an absolutely frustrating experience. Suppose you were getting oral sex from a woman and, right before you were ready to come, she stopped. Imagine the letdown and frustration! And if that's not bad enough, imagine that she starts again and once more stops just before you reach orgasm. This is a common occurrence for females, and it can happen several times during a sexual encounter. Simply put, sex for women can be frustrating, inconvenient, time consuming and messy.

But you said that women put a lot more effort into having affair sex than they do having sex with their husbands.

Yes, females associate preparations for sex with the desire for sex.

I know, but it seems like it would get old pretty quickly. It seems like affair sex would be even more inconvenient than marital sex.

Women typically do not see their affair partners very often, so they continue to get the new-partner, in-love buzz every time. Remember, getting ready for sex is like foreplay for women; they start anticipating the sex long before they ever actually have it. Anticipating sex in an extra-marital affair produces a stimulant buzz. It's like taking amphetamines or doing line after line of coke.

I gather you no longer think that females have a greater biological aversion to familiarity than males.

You're right. I think familiarity affects males and females in similar ways. For some time I also wondered if the problem women have with marital sex might be linked to the duality issue. Just as men categorize women as either "good" or "bad," women tend to see themselves in the same dual framework. The majority of the women I talked to said that they experienced uninhibited sex with their lovers. They felt they were able to express a part of themselves that they didn't feel comfortable expressing with their husbands.

Some people might conclude that wild sex, or even sex in general, conflicts with the "good wife" image, but I don't think that's necessarily the case. Some of the women I talked to were very sexual in the beginning of their marriages. And let's not forget, women can eventually lose interest in having sex with their boyfriends as well—even if they've never lived together. The good/bad girl duality obviously couldn't have existed in societies where extramarital sex was tolerated for both men and women, nor could it have existed in polyandrous societies. Yet, these women were choosing to have sex with multiple partners.

The women I interviewed gave a variety of reasons for their affairs. Some said they didn't feel sexual in the good-wife role. Others said they were married to neglectful husbands. At the same time, many women said they were married to great guys. Regardless of the reasons they gave for their affairs, these women all had one thing in common—their desire and participation in extra-marital affairs. This suggests a biological basis, probably triggered by familiarity.

Some people attribute women's desire for sexual duality as a problem created by men—a natural reaction to the Madonna/whore complex. However, the word *dual* means composed of two parts, and our mating feelings are composed of two parts: attraction, which produces excitement and attachment, which produces security. With the madonna/whore complex, men fulfill both of these needs, needs that are inherent in both sexes, not just males. A few of the women I spoke with recognized that they used their extramarital relationships to create excitement without seriously threatening the security provided by their husbands.

These women had no interest in being with their affair partners on a daily basis because they knew familiarity would diminish their sexual desire and pleasure.

And I now know two things for certain. One, it's a fallacy that women don't have affairs for the sex. A woman has an affair because she wants to feel like a *woman*. She wants to experience and express her sexuality. And, two, it's a fallacy that men *only* have affairs for the sex. Some men have affairs because they want to feel loved. Many men become quite emotionally involved with the women they see outside of marriage.

Then what do you think is responsible for the repulsion women feel toward having sex with their husbands? If the reason isn't biological, what's causing it?

Women are repulsed by having sex with their husbands solely as a means to please their husbands. Males may have difficulty understanding this concept, because they can only have sex if they are aroused. It's hard for men to imagine their bodies being used for someone else's pleasure, although Viagra may have changed that somewhat.

The feelings women experience when having sex solely to satisfy their husbands are probably similar to the feelings men have during a proctologic exam. It's an uncomfortable experience and they look forward to its end.

I use this analogy frequently, because it allows men to understand that during intercourse a woman is allowing her body to be entered by another person, and a certain comfort level is required. A woman's comfort level at having her body entered does not necessarily increase with the regularity or frequency of the act. Her acceptance may actually decrease.

Imagine how men would feel if they continued to receive anal exams regularly and frequently, not out of necessity or for physical pleasure, but simply because their doctors liked to perform them. A man's discomfort during the initial exam, which was performed out of necessity, would escalate to feelings of violation, dread and repulsion.

Women's repulsion toward sex in general, or marital sex in particular, is due to continued sexual encounters with their husbands *or* boyfriends in the absence of sexual pleasure or occasional sexual satisfaction.

And, unfortunately, this pattern of sexual relating is quite common. The pattern often begins with the female seeking commitment. If she is sufficiently motivated she will do whatever it takes to gain a man's commitment, including foregoing sexual pleasure in an effort to please her partner.

Most people mistakenly believe that women require a commitment in order to experience sexual pleasure. This is inaccurate. Females need to feel bonded not committed, which is not the same thing.

Just as a woman can love (feel bonded) to more than one child, she can love (feel bonded) and have sex with more than one male.

Women often experience immense sexual pleasure during affairs that lack commitment, while experiencing little sexual pleasure in their committed relationships.

To please a woman sexually, a man must be willing to devote the time needed to help her feel relaxed and comfortable through conversation and affection *prior* to touching her sexually. This stimulates the release of oxytocin and helps arouse her sexually. Sexual satisfaction is achieved through arousal followed by orgasm, followed by more affection and possibly another orgasm. None of these steps requires a future commitment, but they do require a man's time as well as his desire. Women experience their greatest sexual pleasure with men who enjoy pleasing them sexually.

Males need to be aware that the repercussions of continuing a sexual relationship with a woman who is not achieving sexual satisfaction can be detrimental.

Both sexes experience an increase in oxytocin when they achieve orgasm. Oxytocin works like a bonding agent.[2] The result is obvious: males having orgasms are becoming attached to their partners, while females in the absence of a sufficient amount of touching and orgasms are failing to form similar attachments.

I think this knowledge would definitely increase the desire of men to not only show more affection in their relationships with women, but to satisfy them sexually.

The problem for men is, women aren't always truthful about whether or not they are satisfied, so there's no way for men to really know for sure.

Knowing can be especially difficult in the beginning of a relationship, because a man may have difficulty determining if his partner is experiencing sexual pleasure or merely the exhilaration of striving for an exciting goal.

However, a man's uncertainty can sometimes be an indicator. For instance, when you look back on your affair with Judy, do you have any uncertainty as to whether you satisfied her sexually?

No.

Why? Was it because her pleasure was unmistakable?

Yes, very.

The responses of women in their prime are rarely ambiguous. Unlike younger females, women in their prime typically want sex to always result in orgasm. Women who discount the importance of reaching orgasm are probably not telling the truth. Remember back when you were in your sexual prime. How enjoyable was sex if it didn't end with an orgasm?

Point taken.

I'm not trying to imply that men are to blame for women's lack of sexual pleasure. Ultimately, women are the ones who are responsible.

Unfortunately, I need to get going. But thanks for spending so much time talking to me. This conversation will be continued.

December 15, 2003

Kevin and I got sidetracked today, so I didn't come close to answering his question about the suppressed anger that many women carry into their marriages. I also didn't explain the underlying reasons women are so reluctant to say what they want, one of which is, up until recently it didn't matter what women wanted. And I would be surprised if there are many women today who have not been conditioned to believe that their desires are less important than those of men. Women find it difficult to be happy in their romantic relationships because they have been taught that when it comes to men, they will always get the shit end of the stick. Women don't say what they want because they figure, What's the use? We're not going to get it anyway.

However, lots of women say that they do tell men what they want. As a matter of fact, they tell them repeatedly. But do they really? I suspect that they leave out the most important part, which is: "If you don't give me what I want, I will leave you and get it somewhere else." They leave that part out until they announce they're departure, or demand their husband's departure.

Somewhere along the line we lost sight of the fact that women are viewed as innately selfless due in large part to their second class status. How can doing what you are required to do in order to survive be considered selfless? Women continue to do what they think they must do in order to get what they want from men, whom they mistakenly believe to be ever-elusive. This is why so many women feel as though they've been duped after a few years of marriage. Once the excitement of accomplishing what they thought was a difficult feat wears off, the realization sets in. Women finally understand that all of their giving was nothing more than an attempt to get something in return. It wasn't selfless or loving; it was a little more like ass-kissing. This ugliness in themselves is what women today are struggling to deal with and what many often choose to deny. It wasn't ugly when women didn't have a choice, but now they do have a choice, even though many don't see it that way until after the fact. And much of the see-how-it-feels, it's-my-turn, fuck-you attitude that women have today is due to their not getting the expected payoff—continued excitement over getting and being married.

Chapter 5

The Allure of Affairs

So, how are you doing?

I'm okay. Things at home are pretty much the same, but I'm doing okay.

I take it Tracey's still hasn't told you anything.

No, she just acts cold and looks miserable.

Have you thought about whether or not you can remain committed to your marriage if it turns out Tracey is having, or has had, an affair?

You really think she's seeing someone, don't you?

I think she is Kevin—because she's talking about a separation. Initially I was under the impression that women weren't as apt to leave their marriages for another man as they were for other reasons, but that's not what I think now. The women I interviewed who were seeking separations, or had already separated from their husbands, had experienced at least an attraction to another man. In many cases, the women were either involved in affairs or trying to deal with the aftermath of an affair that had recently ended. And when I interviewed women who were divorced, I learned that their divorces were usually precipitated by an attraction to another man, whether the attraction was acted upon or not. Something involving a man preceded the ending of every single relationship. When women feel the attraction buzz, they get their dream back. The "finding the right man and living happily ever after" dream.

I don't understand why a woman would choose to end her marriage just because she's attracted to another man.

Come on, Kevin. You keep forgetting that you've been on the other side of this. Men and women do it all the time because they think what they're feeling will last. Whether the feeling is security, or excitement, marriage is an attempt to either get or hold on to a certain feeling. Most of us are just feeling-chasers. When we have a feeling we like, we do everything in our power to hold on to it, and if the feeling goes away, we go on a mad chase to try and get it back. That's probably what Tracey is experiencing right now. She's experiencing emotions that she hasn't felt in a long time and she doesn't want to stop experiencing them.

But that feeling *will* go away.

But Tracey probably thinks she is feeling something that she has never felt before.

I think the reason affairs are so hard to stop is because they make us higher than we would be in a normal attraction state. Maybe we get larger doses of brain chemicals, or more chemicals come into play because of the circumstances surrounding the affair. Even in a normal attraction state, we're high enough to make choices that we wouldn't normally make. Think about how many people change the entire course of their lives when they meet someone to whom they're strongly attracted. Yet during an affair people can be so fucked up, they shouldn't even be on the road, much less allowed to make life-altering decisions.

If Tracey is seeing someone, keep in mind that her attraction to the guy is giving her a shot of amphetamine, or to put it more accurately is increasing the rate at which her brain produces PEA. Since she's married, she feels like she can't be with the guy, so she wants him even more. Striving for something or looking forward to something produces a stimulant effect in the brain. I suspect she's constantly looking forward to seeing the guy. Because she's living in a state of fear, her fight-or-flight response is regularly triggered, giving her ongoing adrenaline rushes. The fear of getting caught, the fear of giving up her life with you, and the fear of never again having the feeling she has with the new guy—all of these things are causing changes in her brain chemistry.

With these wide ranging feelings of fear and excitement Tracey could be stoned out of her mind.[1] Though she may believe that she is experiencing something entirely new, in actuality circumstances are just making her feel higher than she has been in the past. Tracey has not been in an attraction state since before the two of you were married. Like a drug addict who quits doing drugs and then, years later, starts up again, the intensity of her feelings may approximate those of her first romantic high.[2] Obviously this would fuel Tracey's belief that she is experiencing something that she has never felt before.

According to the authors of *Craving Ecstasy*, love can be the most difficult of addictions because of "…love's unequaled capacity to profoundly influence each of the three pleasure planes—arousal, satiation, and fantasy…"[3]

Falling in love may not be the high of all highs, but falling in love when you are already married may very well be. Affairs may be the "crack high" of natural acts.

I recall when I was having an affair with Judy. I couldn't think straight. It was the first time in my life that I felt completely out of control.

Almost twenty-five years ago, prior to knowing about its chemical origins, Dorothy Tenov wrote a book titled *Love and Limerence*. She coined the word *limerence* to describe the crazy romantic state you experienced during your affair with Judy. She described limerence as intrusive and obsessive thinking, fantasizing, and acute longing for a specific person. She also explained that "limerent" individuals experience rising and plummeting energy levels—a loss of energy when they are not with their love interest, and an increase in energy prior to and during meetings between the two.

The feelings people experience when they're "limerent" are so intense that everything else in life seems insignificant by comparison. However, it seems that in order to experience limerence, sexual desire must be coupled with uncertainty or fear about the future of the relationship.

In other words, wanting what you can't have.

More accurately, wanting what you *might* be able to have or *could* have if the circumstances were different. This would make simple sexual attractions that happen after marriage fertile grounds for limerence. I used to call it the "if only" syndrome. If only he lived in the same state, if only he weren't married, if only he didn't drink, if only he loved me as much as I love him, if only he treated me better. If only he were a completely different guy, I'd be happy.

People experience varying degrees of limerence. Its intensity increases in direct proportion to the uncertainty or difficulty of developing or sustaining the relationship. Therefore, individual cases of limerence could be branded as mild, moderate or severe. What's fascinating, though, is that the possibility of a relationship has to exist. If circumstances are such that the relationship cannot begin or continue, limerence will not occur or quickly fade. This explains why some people have so much difficulty being direct and straightforward when they try to end a relationship. Many claim that they don't want to hurt the other person's feelings, but most don't want their partner to let go and start getting over them.

Obviously, lots of circumstances can trigger limerence, but most probably don't generate the level of excitement that affairs generate, for several reasons. If an affair develops between two individuals, either or both of whom are married, sexual desire is present along with the improbability that the relationship can develop. However, during an affair, only the circumstances act as barriers; both individuals typically express intense feelings for one another. Affairs provide a safety net that allows men and women to express unrestricted emotion and sexuality, which fuel desire. The natural fear experienced by available single people who find themselves attracted to each other usually produces caution and controlled expression. The circumstances surrounding most affairs, in contrast, create a sense of impossibility, which not only produces intense feelings and desire, but permits individuals to fully express the intensity of their emotions.

Fear and excitement are heightened by the secrecy, the risk, the taboo and the freedom of emotional and sexual expression, as well as by the flood of sexual chemicals and hormones that come into play once the relationship is consummated.

All of these things combined are what make affairs so utterly intoxicating. It's no wonder people often wind up losing everything because of them. But the high isn't the only allure. What also makes affairs unique is their ability to *continue* to intoxicate, producing the highest of highs for indefinite periods of time.

I can't imagine feeling that way indefinitely. I wouldn't want to. It was too crazy for me.

Really? I thought you told me you would have liked to have had both? At the time, wouldn't you have preferred to stay married to Jill, while continuing your affair with Judy?

I know I said that, but I don't think I could have kept it up.

Because you thought it was wrong or because you were afraid it would end?

I'm not sure I know what you mean. Are you asking me if I was afraid of getting caught?

No, that's not what I think you were afraid of. Your situation with Judy had an added fear factor: Judy was single. I think her availability greatly contributed to the craziness you experienced at the time. You were constantly afraid she might meet somebody else and move on. That drove you insane. It made you feel powerless and out of control, because you knew there was nothing you could do about it.

How did you know that? That's all I thought about. It did drive me crazy.

I'm sure it did, as it does most married people who have affairs with single people. From what I've seen, affairs involving a single person with a married person wreak the most havoc.

There's no shortage of advice for single people about the dangers of becoming involved with a married person, but I think there's an even greater need to warn married people about the dangers of getting involved with someone who is single. Married people experience substantially more pain and can remain in pain for much longer periods of time. When they find someone else, single people move on to a new life and another high without missing a beat. But married people must try and resume their old lives while crashing hard with an amphetamine-like withdrawal. And the worst part is, married people have to walk around pretending that nothing is wrong.

I remember once, when Judy and I were seeing each other and I was still married to Jill, I called Judy and she told me she was going out on a date. I can't tell you how badly I felt that day. That's when I made up my mind to do something.

You're lucky. Judy may have been trying to force your hand. It's possible she didn't even have a date. If she had, things might have turned out much differently. When the single partner in an affair decides to start seeing someone else, he or she is usually finished with the affair. Unfortunately, it can trigger a desperate response in the married partner, who, believing the lover would really rather be with them, leaves his or her spouse. In the meantime, the single partner has discovered that there are other drug dealers out there. Someone else can make them feel the attraction buzz.

Yes, but the married person gives them a buzz, so why wouldn't they want to keep seeing the married person?

Because with a new person, they can start from the beginning. The instant people feel the attraction buzz, they realize that they are once again on the edge of a relationship's initial exhilarating stage. The current affair seems old and boring compared to the excitement of starting over again. It's usually devastating to the married person, because of the significance placed on the relationship. During the affair, the married person may have believed that the "right" person or soul mate had finally come along.

Affairs 101: Married people stay the hell away from single people!

Especially single people who live out of town—unless you want to get divorced.

I heard that if you're going to have an affair, you *should* have it out of town.

I interviewed six different people who met someone while they were out of town for meetings or job training. All six eventually got divorced. Two singles meeting out of town can trigger a bad case of limerence, but the difficulty of a married person pursuing an out-of-town affair is insanely greater. Two of the six people I spoke with ended up moving to be with their lovers, but both of the relationships eventually ended.

I have a friend who was married and met a single woman out of town. He ended up getting divorced over it, too. I think his affair lasted almost a year. At one point, she said she was pregnant.

Females frequently use a pregnancy scare to test the commitment of the male they are sleeping with. They throw it out there to see what kind of reaction they get. And sometimes, when they're not on birth control, women let the man decide whether or not to use a condom. If the guy opts *not* to use a condom, women often view it as a sign of commitment.

Women are fucked up.

You wouldn't call a man fucked up because he wanted to spread his sperm, so why call a woman fucked up because she wants to gather it. It's instinctive. Females don't enjoy intercourse as much when the male doesn't ejaculate inside of them. Condoms, as well as the ineffective but popular "pulling out" method can be as unfulfilling to females as they are to males.

I suspect this woman just said that she was pregnant, because later she claimed to have had a miscarriage. To make a long story short, the woman said she would move here as soon as my friend left his wife, but then she said she wouldn't move here until he filed for divorce, and then she said she wasn't coming until the divorce was final. She never did move here. But she did contact my friend's wife and tell her about the affair. A man would never do that—he wouldn't call another man and tell him that he was screwing his wife.

Actually, men would and do. Indulging in this type of behavior is more a personality trait than a gender difference.

I hate to admit it, but I probably would not have divorced Jill if Judy had been married. We probably would have continued having an affair.

I've heard a lot of women say that, too. The married women who had affairs with single men were much more likely to want a separation or divorce than those who had affairs with married men. They didn't just fear their single lover would meet someone else, they didn't want their lover to think badly of them. Some of the women created the impression they were in horrible marriages and planning to leave their husbands. Even when a married woman is having sex with another man in her marriage bed, she will often try to appear virtuous to her lover, fearing that otherwise he will stop seeing her.

One woman had been having an affair with a married man for over six years when she became attracted to and started seeing a single guy. Throughout the original affair, she'd had no intention of divorcing. But the affair with a single man drove her crazy. Had she believed that the single man would continue their affair indefinitely, she would not have divorced. But she believed he would think badly of her for remaining in her marriage.

A couple of women tried a different approach: they fixed up their affair partners with dates. They wanted them to hurry up and get married so they could stop living in fear, assuming that the men would eventually be ready to resume the affair.

We are going to have to continue this conversation later. I've got to pick up the kids. As always, though, I appreciate you talking to me.

And as always, it's no problem.

Jan. 12, 2004

I've never seen Kevin avoid dealing with anything. I know that I shouldn't be surprised by his passiveness. Almost all the men I talked to took the same approach with their wives. But it's just so out of character for him. Kevin told me once that most problems are due to poor decision making. He said people are poor decision makers because they're afraid to make wrong decisions. His financial success is a result of making lots of decisions—some right, some wrong—and that fear never played a role because no single decision could make or break him. I think he was right. Fear keeps people stuck. If Tracey does wind up leaving Kevin, his life will not be permanently altered for the worse. Neither will the lives of his children. The same philosophy Kevin applies to his professional life holds true in his personal life. People, events, and decisions create changes in our lives, but no single, person, event, or decision makes, breaks or defines our lives.

Chapter 6

Why Women Find Affair Sex Particularly Appealing

So, tell me, is there any way to fix this?

Try talking to Tracey again. But when you do, don't be surprised if she still denies that she's seeing someone. I know her denial will make you feel better, but keep in mind that her behavior indicates otherwise. She's telling you she's not happy. She's not giving you any reasons for her unhappiness. She has withdrawn from you emotionally and physically and she thinks the two of you should separate. All of the signs are there. It's natural for you to be in denial, but your denial is a further sign that Tracey is having an affair.

I haven't been in denial. It wasn't until I talked to you that I considered an affair as a possibility.

Exactly. If you weren't in denial, you would most certainly have suspected that something like this could be going on. But in your mind, cheating is something Tracey would never do. If I told you that a man I was seeing was doing the same things that Tracey is doing, you would automatically conclude he was seeing someone else. Your beliefs about Tracey—your image of her— doesn't permit you to see what's really happening. If you allowed yourself to comprehend what's going on, your image of her would change. That's what you're afraid of. People are often in love with their image of another person, the image they carry around in their heads. But an image is fixed, and behavior isn't. For example, several years ago I told you about an emotional affair I was having. You tried to excuse my behavior. You told me not be so hard on myself, that because of my mom's death I really wasn't myself. When I clarified that my mother hadn't become ill until after the affair started, you still wanted to dismiss my behavior.

I remember that. Interestingly, I still think that a lot of your behavior back then was due to your mother's death.

I know you do. You don't want me to take responsibility for my behavior because my behavior at the time didn't match your image of me.

That's true.

And I'm just your friend. So, you see, a man's beliefs about his wife makes dealing with this type of reality somewhat difficult.

What's also difficult is that men usually don't discuss their feelings with anyone *other* than their wives, so they're lost when something like this happens. If men had open, honest friendships with other men, they would learn that many of their friends have gone through this, too. As it stands, a lot of men think they're the only one experiencing this type of marital turmoil.

All you hear in the media are stories about men cheating on women, not vice-versa. The media never portray female infidelity as resulting from normal sexual impulses. Women's affairs are always justified and reasoned away, if they are mentioned at all. I once did an Internet search for articles dealing with women's infidelity. The results listed articles about men cheating on their wives and how women cope. You would think that female infidelity was rare, yet it is as common for women as it is for men, and some have speculated that, today, females may be engaging in extra-marital relationships at a higher rate than males.

Because the focal point has always been the male sex drive and its penchant for variety, females are usually unable to bring their own sexual impulses to awareness. They have always focused their attention on trying to make men faithful. Lack of awareness about their own sex drive increases the likelihood that women will try to justify their affairs by either claiming neglect, or by viewing themselves as victims.

But the media aren't the only ones who guard women's secret. Men do as well by failing to talk about their experiences with infidelity. I would be willing to bet that you have not talked to anyone other than me about this.

No, not a soul.

And yet this has been going on for a long time.

I know. I just keep thinking it's going to get better.

Kevin, if you keep avoiding this, it will get a lot worse. When a woman is trying to end a marriage, she can do some pretty bad things.

What do you mean?

For example, she could let you catch her sleeping with somebody else.

Tracey would never do that.

Kevin, I hate to say it, but the possibility exists. How has she been acting lately?

She's been pretty distant. She seems to want to avoid being around me. Sometimes she looks at me as though she wishes I would just go away.

Remember the information I sent to you about the stages? The women in stage three tried to get their husbands to make the decision to separate so they wouldn't have to. Some of the women couldn't believe the things their husbands were willing to put up with. Initially they thought if they were cold and treated their husbands terribly, the men would leave, or ask them to leave. But typically that's when the man started doing everything in his power to make his wife happy. Often, the woman's behavior kept getting worse.

Why don't women just tell their husbands that they are sleeping with somebody else?

I know you're going to have a hard time believing this, but it's because they don't want to hurt their husband's feelings.

What? So they end up destroying their husband's feelings instead.

Now listen. They *say* they don't want to hurt their husband's feelings, but the truth is, they don't want to feel bad for hurting their husband's feelings. A woman's shame and guilt can be so overwhelming that she doesn't realize she is trying to protect herself from pain, not her husband.

Females are inclined to let males down easy, although their reasons for doing so are quite different today than they were in the past. Until recently, women had to be extremely careful not to arouse male anger and potential violence. It wasn't too long ago that women weren't able to get help from the police if their husbands were physically abusive because the police didn't want to get involved in domestic disputes. I don't think we started seeing significant changes until Nicole Simpson was murdered. So women today may let men down easy in order to avoid remorse, or their behavior could be instinctively self-protective.

Recent research indicates that male and female brains are different in a number of respects. One apparent result is that females are better than males at reading the emotions of others. This natural ability helped early females to ensure their own survival as well as the survival of their offspring. Since males are typically stronger than females, it makes sense for females to have some means other than strength to protect themselves. The ability to tune into the emotions of others not only allows females to anticipate the needs of their offspring, it also equips them to anticipate the behavior of males who could become violent and injure or kill them.

Consequently, females are also more malleable than males. They're more adaptable and it's easier for them to make adjustments in their behavior. However, this doesn't mean they *want* to modify their behavior in order to accommodate the people around them. It just means that they are able to do so with less difficulty than males.

Females try incessantly to please those around them because from the time they're young, shame—the most painful human emotion—is used to control and manipulate their behavior. Females are taught that by behaving in ways that please males, they will also please others around them. Males want them to be innocent, loving, giving and, to ease inherent male paternity insecurity, virtuous and monogamous.

A woman uses pleasing behavior to gain a man's commitment, and she often stops pleasing him in an effort to sever that commitment.

To avoid feeling remorse for telling a man that she wants the relationship to end, a woman will often manipulate the man into thinking he wants it to end.

But why don't women just say what they want? Do they expect men to read their minds?

Yes, that's exactly what they want. Women want men to read their minds—or, more accurately, their emotions—because it's what they do, easily.

I suppose that's why Tracey often says that she shouldn't have to tell me how she feels. I should just know.

Exactly. Females want males to anticipate their needs and desires. Women have the grossly distorted notion that telling men what they want will take all of the joy out of receiving it. This distortion stems from the deep seated belief that males don't really want to be in committed relationships. In the past, hinting and manipulating were the only means by which women could hope to get their needs met, because back then their needs didn't matter.

This pattern of relating has become habitual for females, which is why stating their needs and desires directly is so excruciatingly hard for them.

Due to their inability to anticipate their mate's needs, men are typically unaware that their wives are unhappy until it's too late. However, when a man finally realizes that his wife may leave him, he and his wife often reverse roles. The man becomes the subordinate partner, or the pleaser, in the relationship.

And that's what I've been doing.

You spend the majority of your time thinking about Tracey because you fear that you might be losing her. Right now, you are experiencing what life can be like for females. The fear instilled in females that males cheat and leave them motivates them to be accommodating and attentive, particularly in the beginning of a relationship.

My whole life revolves around trying to make Tracey happy. No matter what I do, nothing seems to work.

That's because you're doing the opposite of what she wants you to do. Many women resort to extreme measures to get their husbands to leave them, but it doesn't always work. Inadvertently, couples get caught in a painful, ugly game of tag that can go on for years. A man's fear combined with his image of his wife blinds him to what his wife is really trying to do.

Many people use this technique to end their relationships. It's not uncommon for a man to treat a woman badly in order to get rid of her. If that doesn't work, he consciously or subconsciously tries to get caught cheating so his wife or girlfriend will end the relationship.

Do you really think that's what Tracey is trying to do?

You said Tracey wants the two of you to separate. Did she say for how long? Does she want to separate for a short time? Is she talking about getting an apartment?

She mentioned getting an apartment.

Is she planning to take the kids with her?

No, right now she says she just needs to get away for a while and sort things out.

I've heard this scenario before. The woman gets an apartment so the kids don't have to be uprooted while she tries out her boyfriend on a more regular basis. I once talked with a man whose wife got an apartment. She rarely visited him or their kids. After three years of separation he still believed that his wife would come back, and that she was sincere when she said, "I'm just trying to find myself." He never once considered that his wife was having an affair. And, like most of the men I talked to, he thought he was solely to blame for his wife leaving. He regularly beat himself up for the things that he thought he had done wrong in the marriage. One night his wife came by to see the kids. While she was there she asked him why he hadn't yet filed for a divorce. She told him that she was never coming back, because she was seeing someone else. Then she described having twice had sex with another man in their bedroom while they were still living together. He was shocked and asked her how she could do this to him. She laughed and asked, "How could you be so stupid not to know?"

After they divorced, he found out that his ex-wife intentionally tried to provoke him into hitting her that night, because she was afraid that abandoning her kids for three years might have jeopardized her chances of gaining custody.

Why did she want custody? It doesn't sound like she really cared whether or not she spent time with her kids.

Probably several reasons. First, she had established a new relationship so she didn't need as much freedom as when she was trying to find and cultivate one. She also made considerably more money than he did and didn't want to pay child support. Having custody also gave her a measure of control. To this day, she never has the kids ready when he is scheduled to pick them up, but he's afraid to take legal action. He doesn't have the money she has and thinks the courts always favor the mother.

How often do women provoke men to hit them in order to get what they want in a divorce?

Two women I talked with admitted to that. Both knew that the men they intentionally provoked would never have hurt them. They did it to enhance their advantage in the divorce. However, some women try to provoke their husbands as a means of justifying their own behavior.

At least one man I interviewed saw through his wife's behavior. After 15 years of marriage, she announced one day that she had met her "soul mate" and told him that she wanted him to move out of their house.

Did he do it?

No, that's what's so funny. He told her that if she wasn't happy, *she* should move out, because he wasn't leaving his kids. She said, "Okay, but you need to know that my boyfriend will be here on Tuesdays and Thursdays, so I don't want you to come home on those days."

You're kidding.

It gets worse. Obviously, the wife thought that he would leave rather than accept her conditions. One morning about a month later his wife walked into the kitchen and noticed that he had tears in his eyes. She looked at him and said, "God, Dan, get over it. Quit being so pathetic." He couldn't believe how cold and insensitive she was. He was blown away by the whole thing, but fortunately he knew his rights as a parent and homeowner.

What happened? What did he do?

He agreed not to come home on Tuesdays and Thursdays. He spent those nights at his brother's house. But one Tuesday morning, he called and told his wife that he needed to stop by after work and pick up something he'd forgotten. He wanted to give her ample warning that he was going to be there for a couple of minutes on one of his banished days. When he got there, candles were lit all over the house and his wife was wearing a teddy.

Did she want to have sex with him?

No. She told him to hurry up and get what he needed and get out, because her boyfriend was on his way over. She started taunting him about her impending evening. He had a feeling she was baiting him, that she wanted him to do something. He'd had that feeling more than once while they were still living together, but on this particular night he was sure that she was trying to provoke him.

Was she successful?

No. He didn't do anything. But he wound up getting the house and joint custody, which is rare if my interviews are a fair indication. He was lucky, though. His wife told him what she was doing. In the majority of the stories I've heard, the men were oblivious to their wives' affairs until after the marriages ended. He was spared the additional pain of living in limbo for one or more years, as many people do. However, some women I interviewed did leave their marriages rather abruptly.

I just can't believe any of these things might be happening with Tracey.

Kevin, I know it's hard, but try and be open-minded about Tracey's behavior. What would you think if I told you the same story about someone I was seeing? If I said that my live-in boyfriend wanted to get his own apartment, would you think he was seeing someone, or would you think he was trying to work on our relationship?

I know. I know. I would think he was seeing somebody.

If you don't deal with this, it's going to get a lot worse. For instance, Tracey has been telling you that in order to stay married she needs to separate from you. And you're not planning on doing anything. You're just waiting to see what happens.

What else can I do? I can't make her stay.

The part of marriage that nobody ever talks about is separation: the beginning of the end of a marriage. This situation with Tracey could go on for a couple of years. In breaking her attachment bond with you, she may wait to act until she thinks you are okay. She wants you to get you used to being apart from her.

The women I spoke with were surprised by how devastated their husbands were when the women tried to leave, so many dragged out the process in hopes of making it easier. Some men tried to take advantage of their wives' feelings of guilt, but trust me, it didn't keep their wives from eventually leaving, nor did it stop them from sleeping with somebody else. Tracey has probably been trying to get you to end the relationship. Since you haven't, she may begin to take drastic measures. Each of you is manipulating the other in order to get what you want.

I'm not trying to manipulate her. I just want her to be happy!

You say you want Tracey to be happy, but the truth is you don't want her to leave you. That's why you are trying so hard to please her. The women I spoke with grew angry when their husbands became over-attentive in an effort to keep them from leaving. Many of the women were quite accommodating during the initial stages of their relationship. During the first few years of their marriage most of the women got caught up in creating an image of the perfect wife, the perfect home and the perfect family. They resented workload imbalances between themselves and their husbands, but pushed those feelings aside. On the few occasions when they did express their anger, they felt guilty. Many women said they regularly vacillated between feelings of *anger* and *guilt* in their relationships. Their pleasing and accommodating behavior early in the relationship was an effort to get the guy and live out their fantasy.

The women began to express their anger right around the time changes in their body chemistry made them feel more independent and assertive, or when they got a new job and felt that they no longer needed their husband, or when they became attracted to another man. For women who had felt so needy in the past, the feelings of independence were exhilarating.

Try to see the similarities between your behavior right now and Tracey's behavior near the beginning of your relationship. You are altering your behavior in order to get Tracey to stay. You're scared, and your *fear* is motivating you to do the *opposite* of what needs to be done. Kevin, you can't make Tracey happy and neither can anyone else. The sooner you realize that the better.

What do you mean when you say I'm doing the opposite of what needs to be done? What needs to be done?

You need to wake up and quit avoiding the problem. You need to quit acting as if kissing Tracey's ass is going to change your situation. You need to get over your fear of Tracey's leaving you. I know it's a lot easier said than done, but I assure you, this could go on for a long time if you don't find the courage to deal with it.

Another reason the women I interviewed became so angry when their husbands started bending over backwards to make them happy is it made them feel guiltier. Many had already made their decision to leave long before their husband got wind of the idea, so when their husband became Mr. Wonderful their guilt over leaving increased and was expressed as anger. The pleasing behavior turned them off, because they were accustomed to being "pleasers" and knew pleasing was a form of manipulation. When the husbands continued to ignore their wives cold, distant and sometimes abhorrent behavior, their failure to respond proved how out of touch they were with their feelings.

But I don't understand. Tracey and I haven't had a bad marriage, we've had a really good marriage.

Even men and women in happy marriages are vulnerable at times to the urgings of their sex drives, particularly if they don't understand them, which is the case for many women.

The difference between men who cheat on their wives and women who cheat on their husbands is, men are likely to blame their infidelity on a powerful sex drive while women are likely to blame their infidelity on the husband. Both are trying to maintain an image of themselves that fits the images society promotes of acceptable male and female behavior.

If Tracey is having an affair, wouldn't you rather believe she is cheating because of something you've done, rather than believe that she is acting on sexual impulses?

I really don't know how I feel about anything right now.

You read about the stages that women go through. Well, men also go through stages as they try to deal with their wives leaving them. I have talked with people who have been intermittently or continuously separated for up to seven years. The men usually just waited for their wives to come back. They were in shock. Many experienced a paralyzing fear. They were afraid that anything they did might push their wives to divorce them. The women, by contrast, initially thought their husbands would make the decision to divorce, but rather quickly sensed their husband's fear and realized that he wasn't going to leave them—or do much of anything, for that matter. Many of the men became suicidal when their wife left and remained so for a long time afterwards. A few of the men said that they felt homicidal. They didn't want to kill themselves, they wanted to kill somebody else.

Most of the men didn't have anyone to talk to other than their wives, which is why I believe they tried so desperately to hold on to them. The devotion and accommodating behavior that many of the wives exhibited in the beginning of their relationships helped to create an unhealthy dependency in the men. Some of the men were so dependent on their wives, they didn't think they could live without them, but one thing all of the men shared was a fear of losing their children.

I'm not losing my kids! I don't want to live without them. How the hell can a woman do this? That's why men put up with the way their wives treat them—because they're afraid she'll take the kids!

For the men I talked with, it was a combination. They didn't want to lose their children, and they didn't want to lose the only person they felt close to. Some of the stories I heard were unbelievable. I never imaged that so many men have such similar stories to tell. Yet we seldom hear this side of the story, unless it's to justify the cheating and the leaving, or to portray it as a rarity. I think it's another strategy to control female sexuality.

How so?

Female infidelity has always been judged much more harshly than male infidelity, in part because so few stories on the subject are told. The lack of stories about female infidelity perpetuates the belief that it rarely happens. I think the deception is intentional. If stories of women's infidelity appeared regularly in the media, they would undermine the belief that female infidelity is unnatural and diminish the effectiveness of shame as a sexual deterrent.

And it keeps men from talking, because they're too embarrassed to admit that it has happened to them.

Exactly.

You said some people live this way for years. How is that possible? I don't see myself putting up with it for very long. I couldn't take it. This is all I think about and it's driving me crazy!

Kevin, your wife doesn't have sex with you. She never shows you any affection. Now you are about to agree to live in separate houses. Your behavior is no different from the other men I talked to. Their image of their wives didn't allow them to see what was going on.

I talked to men who found other men's clothing in the house. Some found e-mails. I talked to one guy whose wife was having an affair with her boss. She was subpoenaed to testify at the boss's divorce hearing. Instead of realizing that his wife was cheating, he concluded that the boss was married to a nut case. Not one of these men questioned the wife's excuses. Only in hindsight, *after* their divorce did they recognize any signs of infidelity.

One guy's wife, after a two year separation, refused to finalize their divorce until he agreed that he would never allow any woman he was seeing to spend the night at his house while their kids were there. Throughout the separation she was very jealous and continued to claim that she just needed time to "find herself." She got married three weeks after they divorced. At the time I interviewed this guy he had been seeing the same woman for a little over a year, but unless he married her she couldn't stay the night at his house while his children were there. Yet his wife moved another man into her house three weeks after the divorce.

Men are stupid.

No, men aren't stupid. The men I talked to were just convinced that cheating was something their wife would never do. Women cheat with less difficulty than men because we assume they won't. That trust affords them more opportunities.

The men I interviewed trusted their wives. Their wives came and went as they pleased, rarely provoking the suspicion and interrogations regularly encountered by the men. Some of the husbands learned to look down in restaurants and other public places, because they feared their wife would accuse them of looking at another woman. Some claimed that their wife didn't want them to watch certain television programs.

I know what that's like. Tracey is always giving me the third degree.

Most of the women I talked with had no trouble getting away from the house. They would say they were going to the grocery store or running to the mall, and their husband never suspected a thing. That's an advantage women have because of the double standard. One woman I interviewed met her lover before church on Sunday mornings. Do you think her husband suspected that she was having an affair?

At first, some of the women resented their husbands' lack of suspicion—his assumption that they would never cheat. The women thought their husbands were clueless. They didn't like that their husbands were taking their fidelity for granted. But that was only in the beginning, when the affairs first started. Later, they liked having the freedom.

The double standard poses two major disadvantages for men. First, men who believe that women want to get married and are naturally monogamous might be inclined to put less effort into their marriages. Second, men who think they have to give up a lot when they marry might have an increased level of commitment compared to women who mistakenly believe they're not giving up anything.

You said that men go through stages. What are they?

Well, you are in the first stage. The men I talked to who were in this stage felt lost. They did everything they could to make their wives happy and they blamed themselves for all the problems. They had difficulty working, they couldn't sleep and they usually lost considerable weight. Several experienced vomiting or panic attacks. Basically, their lives stopped.

Kevin, you need to get to the truth about what's going on *before* you and Tracey separate. Otherwise you can't reach a resolution. You'll be stuck. The pain of separation is often similar to the pain people feel when a loved one has gone missing. People in that situation can't move through the grieving process because their loved one might still be alive, so they fluctuate between hope and fear. Imagine living in fear of Tracey's leaving you for a year, two years or more.

I can't imagine hanging on for that long. If Tracey moves out and doesn't show any signs of wanting to move back, I'll move on.

That's part of the problem. Most of the men I interviewed were unable to move on, because their wives kept giving them mixed signals.

That's all I've been getting from Tracey—mixed signals.

You are probably going to keep getting them. Tracey's pain over leaving is causing a lot of confusion. She probably cries whenever she talks about leaving, and you interpret her tears as a desire to stay.

But I don't understand why she would do something that causes her that much pain. It doesn't make sense.

It makes perfect sense if you take into consideration that she is torn between two things.

All right, I get it. Just tell me what I can expect next, because it sounds as though stage one for men consists of pain and denial.

In Stage 2, the men continued to experience the same feelings they experienced in Stage 1, only a woman almost always entered the picture. The majority of the men said that they made it through the separation and, in some cases, the period leading up to the separation because of a woman who entered the picture at that time.

So, the men started having affairs?

Yes, but the affairs were usually mired in the man's grief. In a few cases, the man was unable to have sexual relationships with the woman he started seeing.

Why, because he felt guilty?

These man were in a lot of pain. They were emotionally overwrought. Some couldn't get an erection. It's not uncommon for a man to have sexual problems after separating from someone he has been with for a long time. The men developed these relationships so they could have someone to talk to. Most said that having an affair was the last thing on their minds at the time, but they didn't know what else to do. They felt lonely and isolated. Most of them talked about having very low self-esteem due to their wife's emotional coldness and repeated sexual rejection. Many men credited the woman who helped them with saving their lives, which may be a literal truth.

The men I iinterviewed feared losing their family, but the women didn't seem to have that fear. The women thought of it as losing their husband, not their family. More often than not, the men were forced to move out of their homes and away from their kids. They lost all of their attachment bonds and felt as though they were losing their whole identity.

This just isn't right.

Divorce can be very unfair to men. Yet women are usually perceived to be the victims of divorce.

I realize that the men you talked to were traumatized over losing their families, but I still don't see how they could sit back and let their wives walk all over them.

To say they were in pain is an understatement. Breaking attachment bonds is like going through heroin or morphine withdrawal. That's what men, women and children can go through during a divorce—a narcotic withdrawal.

But it wasn't just the pain. Other factors caused the men to handle the situation ineffectively. Remember, these men were oblivious to what their wives were doing. They thought of their wives in the same way you think of Tracey. They felt powerless during divorce proceedings because they were still hoping that the wife would change her mind and didn't want to do anything to jeopardize a possible reconciliation. Most of the men also knew that divorce laws typically favor the mother.

Let's back up for a minute. You said breaking attachment bonds is like going through heroin or morphine withdrawal. Why weren't the women going through withdrawal?

They were, but withdrawal is easier when an individual has one or more intact attachment bonds or is "high" on a new partner. Also, the women usually felt quite bonded to their lovers due to the touching and orgasms they were experiencing in their affairs, resulting in increased levels of oxytocin, the bonding molecule. A woman involved in an affair, though suffering, has no idea how much pain her spouse and children are in. The affair acts as an anti-depressant, masking her pain. She will typically grieve much later, possibly several years down the road.

That's what happened to me. By the time I realized what I had done to Jill, it was too late. She was long past the pain, but for me it was just starting.

I've heard several people say that. They wish they could go back and change the outcome. They didn't realize what they were doing at the time. I'll never forget this one woman I interviewed. She had an affair and eventually married her best friend's husband. The two women had been friends for over fifteen years. When I interviewed her, she had been married to her ex-best friend's ex-husband for eight years and she still couldn't forgive herself.

I remember waking up one day and feeling like a fool. I couldn't believe all the things that I had done. It was like I was temporarily crazy or something.

People coming down from being "on love" feel like they would after a night of heavy drinking. They wake up realizing that they did and said a lot of stupid things. If the euphoric feelings of being "on love" began to diminish earlier, before we'd had frequent and consistent contact with a person, affairs wouldn't be so destructive. I interviewed two women who had long-term affairs with married co-workers. These women saw their lovers every day at work. Both women eventually ended the affair. The sex became boring—not much different from having sex with their husbands. Because they saw their lovers daily, the excitement eventually waned.

So, they were just interested in the sex.

In the beginning both women viewed their lovers as soul mates. However, as time went on their perceptions changed. First they felt guilt, then anger at their husbands. Eventually they felt they needed to make a choice. However, both decided to stay married and continue the infidelity until the affairs died a natural death. Affairs usually keep sex exciting for a long period of time. But when the thrill is gone, the affair usually ends. Both men and women often think that if they leave their spouses for their lovers, the sex with their lovers will continue to be as good as it was during the affair.

However, during an affair, women usually become more aware of their own sexuality. In fact, affairs are quite conducive to female sexual pleasure. Remember when I told you that women love affair sex?

Having an affair keeps desire high, which can benefit a woman in two ways. The inordinate amount of desire renders men much more capable of pleasing women sexually. Remember, women want more sex per sitting, which affairs usually provide. Men spend more time trying to arouse them during an affair, much as they do in the beginning stages of a romantic relationship, when they experience increased desire. Once the desire levels off, sex becomes less satisfying to females due to decreased touching and subsequent orgasms. Women are much more sexual than most people think. If you want to know the truth, it can be difficult for one man to sexually satisfy a woman.

What is that supposed to mean?

When a man has a sexual encounter with a woman, even if he does everything the woman likes—talking, foreplay, and intercourse—afterwards, the man is usually satisfied (unless he's eighteen), but the woman is just getting warmed up. As I've explained before, women can be just as aroused after having sex as they are prior to having sex.

Many of the women I talked to said that, prior to their affairs, sex left them feeling empty. This emptiness wasn't just due to a lack of emotional connection or affection; it was due to a lack of satisfaction. Many women didn't know why they felt unfulfilled. They just knew that something was missing. When they had affairs, they realized what that something was.

Females are physically capable of having sex several consecutive times. One female has the ability to please many males, but a male can have difficulty satisfying just one female, except possibly at the beginning of a relationship or during an affair. During affairs, whether men and women get together once a week, every two weeks, or once a month, they are likely to spend a couple of hours talking, touching, having sex and possibly repeating the process. The majority of the women I interviewed said they had never before experienced the level of sexual pleasure that they experienced in their affairs.

I recall Judy saying that. Most of our time together was spent in bed.

That's what women like—two or more hours of complete and undivided physical and emotional attention. Most women probably would not continue an affair with a man who didn't regularly devote a couple of hours to them and much of that time would be spent in bed. Even though many of the women I spoke with claimed to have found their soul mates, it was obvious from listening to them that sex played a huge role in their extra-marital relationships.

Do women ever fantasize about having sex with more than one guy?

A few women did mention fantasies about being with more than one man. They wanted all their erogenous zones stimulated simultaneously. One woman said she wanted a man on each breast and one between her legs, and another woman said that she wanted one man in front of her and another behind.

Yes, but men want to live out their fantasies, whereas women are satisfied with just keeping their fantasies as fantasies.

Some women do fulfill their fantasies of being with two or more men at a time.

Yeah, but those women are usually sluts.

I really do pray you don't die an idiot.

Why did you say that?

You just said that women don't want to live out their fantasies. Yet, when I mentioned that some women do, you responded that those women are sluts. Don't you see? Some women never execute their fantasies because of what people will think. Many won't admit to having fantasies for the same reason. I'll take it a step further. Many women are unable to *have* sexual fantasies because of the shame involved in doing so.

Our relationship problems will never be resolved until we see an end to the sexual double standard. Whether males are ready for it or not, that time is almost here. I mentioned to you once that if females everywhere stood up and said, "Guess what, we all do," the sex game would be over. Well, that's what's happening. Girls and women are engaging in a lot more sex and with a lot more partners than they did in the past.

The sexual double standard can only exist if females allow it. Males will never decide that it's unfair. It will end when females turn a deaf ear to any and all attempts at sexual shame. One of the things that angered me when I watched the Dr. Phil show on teens and sex was Dr. Phil's statement: "And that's what we're talking about, how to prevent your daughter from having oral sex that first time, how to get her to understand that if you choose the action, you choose the consequences."

If shame is a consequence, its one that females control. As I have heard Dr. Phil say on more than one occasion, "You teach people how to treat you." And as long as women allow shame to manipulate their sexual behavior, society will continue to use shame to control their sexuality. Before long, girls and women alike will no longer feel they have to deny, explain or defend their sexual behavior.

Do you think we should teach kids to have sex with whomever they want? I don't want my daughters getting pregnant or catching some disease!

People try to postpone and limit their kids' sexual encounters by romanticizing the "right one" myth, or by scaring them with the threat of catching a disease. But let's be honest, even if kids just wanted to masturbate with their boyfriends or girlfriends, people would say it was wrong. So, it's not pregnancy or disease that people are worried about, it's sex. And I notice you didn't mention anything about your son. Aren't you worried about him catching a disease or getting someone pregnant?

I don't think you understand. Boys use girls for sex. I want to try and protect my daughters from that—I don't want them to have to find out the hard way.

No, I don't think *you* get it. Girls like sex! We teach girls that males only want them for sex. We teach them that sex is something they do for males and it isn't true. A woman's every sexual encounter can be shrouded in the fear that she is being used, which only impedes her ability to understand and enjoy her sexuality, not to mention hindering her ability to choose sexual partners by using her own instinct and intuition. One of the most ridiculous things we still teach girls is that sex is a gift that females give to males. The purpose of this belief is to make females think that they are giving something away or losing something when they have sex. We don't teach these things to protect females from males. These teachings are intended to keep females from accumulating numerous sexual partners, thereby lowering their value. Now, you tell me: what's the difference between what we do and what less civilized societies do? The only difference between punishment, removal of the clitoris, and what we teach is physical pain. The objective is the same—to keep females from having and enjoying sex. Our method may be more civilized, but it's covert and primitive. Ours is still a system where females are the givers (lose something) and males the takers (gain something). It's a system that doesn't allow for females to experience true sexual pleasure.

You *do* think we should teach kids to have sex with whomever they want, don't you?

I think we should *teach* kids. We should share what we know without the hidden intent to control or manipulate their behavior.

What the hell does that mean? That doesn't tell me anything.

We currently teach kids what we want them to know, which is not necessarily the truth. At the very least, we fail to teach them the whole truth. We teach kids in the same way companies sell their products; information is omitted, exaggerated, or created with the intent to get the customer to do what we want them to do. So, to answer your question, I think we should teach kids about sex without omitting, exaggerating, or creating information. But I also think you should sell products that way, too.

But what is the truth? Who knows what the truth is?

The truth is, females lose nothing from having sex and they enjoy having sex, especially when they're not focused on pleasing males. Even though things aren't nearly as bad as they used to be, we still operate under the belief that sex diminishes the value of females while it increases the value of males. If our beliefs about sex and relationships don't completely change, males will continue seeking sex as a sport and females will continue seeking commitment as a sport.

Quite frankly, our cultural beliefs help to eliminate the pressure felt by males as well as encourage them to use females. Do you really think boys would be so eager to have sex if their reputation and self-esteem were at stake with each and every one of their sexual encounters? When a boy goes out with a girl, the only question asked by his peers is, "Did you fuck her?" What if instead the only question asked was, "Did she have an orgasm?"

Imagine if girls returned to school after having sex with boys and announced the size of the boy's penis and publicized the boy's ability or inability to bring her to orgasm. Trust me, boys using girls for sex would quickly become a thing of the past. As a matter of fact, it would be impossible for boys to use girls sexually if girls only had sex for their own sexual pleasure.

Girls and women pursue relationships with boys and men because they think males aren't interested in having relationships. It isn't uncommon for a female to pursue a commitment from a male she doesn't even like, much less want to spend the rest of her life with. Many females don't even know how to receive kindness or love from males. More often than not they believe longing is the primary component in love.

Even though I focused on married women who were having affairs, I did occasionally interview single women. Listen to what a couple of the single females had to say about the males with whom they were involved. One woman had been dating her boyfriend for a year and a half and she desperately wanted to marry him. During our interview she said, "We really don't have that much in common. I don't like how much he drinks and we really don't have very good sex, but I love him." Another woman said, "He treats me like shit and he never wants to spend time with me. Our whole relationship is about him." I asked this woman if the sex was good, because

I thought maybe that was why she stayed in the relationship. She replied, "The sex is terrible. He won't touch me. If I want to get off, I have to get myself off."

This particular woman was beautiful. She would have a difficult time finding a man who *wouldn't* like to be with her. At the end of our conversation I asked her why she wanted to marry the guy and she said, "Because I love him."

Both of these women, if they haven't already, will probably wind up marrying the men they were with at the time I interviewed them. And both women will probably not only divorce these men, they will blame the men for causing the divorce, even though throughout their courtship they continuously professed and ultimately convinced the men of their love. Although these women might label themselves, "women who love too much," the truth of the matter is, they don't love these men. They love the pursuit. When we stop sympathizing with women in similar situations, we'll start to see some change. Once women realize that they often chase after commitment in the same way that men chase after sex—pursue and discard—women will stop seeing themselves as victims and will start taking responsibility for their choices.

Are you saying that you don't think women are even aware that they do this?

No, they often are not aware because of their narrow focus and determination in achieving their goal. However, occasionally women are aware of what they are doing. Unfortunately though, their overall beliefs about males and their bad behavior enable women to justify their own irresponsibility.

I'll stop by again next week so you can finish telling me about the stages that men go through. I want to know what happens after men start having affairs.

Okay, that's fine.

January 19, 2004

Why don't people get it? Why don't they see that many problems of women are rooted in the suppression of their sexuality. This is where their guilt and anger begin and what causes them to continually vacillate between the two emotions. Isn't vacillating between guilt and anger the same as vacillating between hating yourself and hating someone else? Do I hate me or do I hate you?

Why didn't Dr. Phil tell the girls on his show that if they have sex, they should make sure that the guys bring them to orgasm before they give a blow job or agree to intercourse? Imagine the response a comment like that would get from his audience! No, that couldn't happen. A suggestion like that might take power away from the boys. The parents of girls would be outraged. Their beliefs about their daughters' "worth" are no different than society's beliefs. Parents everywhere would be concerned about their daughters "losing value."

If you suppress your sexual desire, you'll feel good about yourself, said the girl on the Dr. Phil show. If you say no, you're going to feel like the best person in the whole world. So in other words, young females get to feel good about themselves provided they don't follow their sexual instincts, whereas males get to feel good about themselves if they do. To say that this double standard makes females angry is an understatement. It's infuriating. But unfortunately, indulging their sexual desires makes them feel guilty. Hence, they vacillate between guilt and anger in all areas of their lives.

If only females realized that they are responsible for the continuance of the sexual double standard. Society can't make females feel guilty. Females can only allow society to make them feel guilty. Males don't need to fear that their sexually-willing girlfriends will give it up to just anyone. They will only give it up to attractive males who can get them off. Ooh, I sound angry. And here I thought I was past all that.

Maybe my anger has something to do with the fact that I've just finished reading the second of two books in a month that strongly advises women to wait to have sex with males. One book was written by a man and the other by a woman. The female author advises women to wait so that the man will become attached to her prior to having sex with him, thereby tricking the man into attachment and, hopefully, commitment. What's the message to women? A man doesn't really want to be in a relationship with you. You're going to have to trick the dumb bastard into being with you.

The male author, however, has a different reason for women to hold out on sex. He says women should wait simply because men want them to. He says a man wants to believe, even if it's not true, that the woman he likes is difficult to get into bed. He does acknowledge that it makes some women angry to play this waiting game. However, the message for those women seems to be, "Tough shit! Wait anyway." If you want a man that's what you're going to have to do.

Obviously this author doesn't get it. Women's anger over advice like this is an indication that they're becoming less and less willing to heed this type of advice. Women are losing interest in pretending. They no longer want to play the role they were forced to play in the past.

Advising women to play the waiting game is detrimental to males, too. It curtails their growth and insults their intelligence. Society can continue to try to convince females that it is they who wish to marry, but eventually even society won't be able to ignore women's behavior or the statistics, which prove unequivocally that it is men, not women, who wish to be married.

Females are tired of remaining silent while taking assaults to their pride and pretending not to have desires similar to those of arrogant, boastful males.

If males continue to taunt females with their we-can-and-you-can't attitude, females will eventually confront their greatest fear (indeed, many are doing so today) and simply say, "Who gives a fuck. We're having sex. And who cares if you don't want to see us again because—guys, are you listening?—we get bored fucking the same person, too."

I wonder if this is what underlies a woman's love of affair sex. During an affair, a woman may for the very first time in her life have sex for no reason other than pleasure. She's not having sex to please the man, with the hope of snagging him, nor is she having sex to keep him. She's also not suppressing or controlling her desire so that he forms the appropriate opinion of her. She's having sex for one reason and that's to experience sexual pleasure. If sex really isn't that important to women, then why are they willing to give up everything for it?

Chapter 7

Women Aren't Just Angry They Want Revenge

I know you want to talk about what happened after the men I interviewed started having affairs, but I think it's important that we spend some time talking about women's anger. It's impossible for you to understand anything about women in this country today, unless you understand that a) they're angry, and b) their anger is directed at men. Women today aren't seeking equality. They want retribution—revenge. I've come a long way in dealing with my own anger, but to say I've overcome it would be a lie. It's something that I still have to deal with regularly.

You've never struck me as being angry at men.

Well, it's true. It sounds terrible, but there was a time when I felt women deserved their "little secret." I thought that because of all the shit women had been through for the last couple thousand years, it was the least they deserved.

There were several things that helped me see things from a different perspective, but one thing in particular caused a dramatic shift in my thinking.

The day after the O. J. Simpson trial, I gave a presentation to a class of African American students. At the end of my presentation, some of the students were talking about the verdict. They were happy that O. J. was found innocent; however, the students didn't *believe* he was innocent, they were just happy he got off. I went home that day feeling horrible. I just couldn't understand how the students could feel that way. The next time I saw my friend Lawrence, I talked to him about it. Lawrence said he thought O. J. was guilty too, but just like the kids in the classroom that day he was happy that O. J. was acquitted. He thought it was funny. He laughed and said, "O. J. beat the system." I was stunned when he said it.

I didn't know it at the time, but later I found out that the way Lawrence felt about white people was similar to the way that I felt about men.

It was four years into my research when I started interviewing men. Prior to that, whenever I would hear men boast about their sexual appetite and sexual conquests, I would laugh on the inside. Once, while I was listening to a male acquaintance brag about a woman at his job that he wanted to sleep with, I took pleasure in knowing that while he was thinking about sleeping with a woman at his job, his wife actually *was* sleeping with a man at her job and had been for some time. I knew because I interviewed her.

But then I started hearing the other side to the story. When I look back now, I wonder why it took me so long to acknowledge that there are two sides to the story. I'll never forget this one man I met. His wife had just left him, and I listened to him talk for a little while. He said, "I waited until I was older to get married. My wife and kids were my priority. I thought I did everything right. I don't understand." As I got up to leave, I told him it wasn't his fault. He looked at me with tears in his eyes and said, "That's what my mom said. What do you mean it's not my fault? What didn't my mom say—what aren't you saying? What isn't my wife telling me? I just want to understand. What piece of the puzzle am I missing?"

What did he say when you explained it to him?

That's the thing. I left without telling him anything. I didn't want to talk about the subject anymore. I felt that I had found the answers I was looking for and wanted to put that part of my life behind me. But after I got home that night, I couldn't get the guy out of my mind. I kept thinking, why didn't I talk to him? It wouldn't have killed me to talk about it one more time.

Shortly after that, I started interviewing men. One of my first interviews was with a guy whose story really tore my heart out. This man had gotten a vasectomy because his wife wouldn't have sex with him; she had told him that she didn't want to risk getting pregnant again. The day he came home from the hospital, he found an e-mail from his wife's boyfriend. It turned out his wife didn't want to risk getting pregnant by her husband because her boyfriend, who'd had a vasectomy, was under the impression that the woman was no longer sleeping with her husband. Even after four years the guy couldn't imagine ever being with a woman again. He was still traumatized by the experience.

Around that same time, the topic of women and their loss of sexual desire started showing up in the media. That's when I decided to write the information booklet. I knew that many women hadn't really lost their sexual desire. I was still very angry at the time, but didn't know to what degree. I just thought if I wrote about it I wouldn't have to talk about it. At that time I was being contacted regularly by people who had heard from either a friend or an acquaintance about my interest in this particular topic. I thought that I could share information with people but avoid getting into lengthy conversations by putting something on paper.

But it was the responses of women to my writings that made me recognize my own anger and that of other women today. Whenever women read my material, they laughed and gave me a high-five.

They did?

Yes. If no one else was around, that's what typically happened when I shared the information with a woman.

One day it hit me how angry I had been. Prior to interviewing men, I was amused by much of the information I gathered. I was amused because I thought that women were *secretly* beating the system. But when I started interviewing men I became aware of the similarities between my feelings and Lawrence's. I understood why women were laughing and giving me high-fives. They were laughing just as I had laughed before I started hearing and seeing the other side to the story.

Regardless of gender or race, it's natural for oppressed people to be angry, defensive, prideful, vengeful, and to feel a sense of entitlement when the oppression subsides. Especially since the oppression doesn't usually stop because the oppressors realize it is wrong, but for some other reason. And, of course, initially the oppressed don't get equal rights, they get *some* rights and have to fight for the rest.

So you're saying women are pissed off.

That's exactly what I'm saying. The men that I talked to often used the word *evil* to describe the behavior of their wives. I think when women decide to leave their husbands, all the pain from their past together with all the pain that women have suffered at the hands of men throughout history is unleashed on their husbands in the form of anger, regardless of whether or not their husbands have treated them badly.

In *Divorced Dads*, the authors bring up the issue of women's anger. They make an interesting point. Listen to what they say, "...Men recovered from their anger at their ex-spouse significantly earlier than women did. This gender difference in recovery from anger may seem paradoxical, in that men are the ones who are most often left, while women more often sought the divorce, and thus obtained the outcome they wanted. One would think, therefore, that men would continue to be angrier longer. While my results, as well as others', appear reliable, there is no definitive study that explains why the paradox occurs. One possibility is what has been called the shattered dreams theory. According to this notion, wives are enraged that their husbands behaved during the marriage in ways that caused the wife to terminate the marriage, shattering her dreams for the future."[1]

For a few years now, I've been trying to understand why women seem unable to get over their anger. I've noticed that once a woman reaches a certain point, not only does her anger persist, she wants to continually punish and inflict pain on whomever angered her.

I've noticed that about women, too.

But the shattered-dreams theory doesn't explain the anger of those women I interviewed whose ex-husbands had treated them reasonably well during the marriage.

I think several factors contribute to the anger of women. One is their collective experience.

Women in the U.S. are no longer automatically subordinate to men, but reminders of the past and of the current degradation of women in many parts of the world abound. Those reminders can cause extreme anger in women and, unfortunately, marriage itself is at times an unpleasant reminder of the subordination inflicted upon females in the past.

Think about some of our traditions and how they originated. For example, the father still gives away the bride. Why do you think we have such a custom? Looking at other cultures suggests its origins. Even today, in some places in the world, females are considered mere property. In some cultures, females are worth money and men sell their daughters. In other cultures females are considered a worthless burden so families pay men to marry them. I suspect that the tradition of the father giving away the bride, as well as the tradition of the bride's parents paying for the wedding, have similar origins.

But that's not how it is now. Those customs are not intended to demean women in any way.

Then why do we practice them?

They're traditions.

Imagine that you are an African-American male who has all the freedoms of an Anglo-American male. However, for some unknown reason, you were brought up to address white males as *sir*, while white males were brought up to address black males as *boy*. It's customary and you think nothing of it until the day you find out that the custom is born of slavery. Tell me, would you still address white males as sir and would you ever again allow a white male to call you *boy*?

That's how some of our customs and traditions affect women. For many women, marriage carries reminders of subordination. Many are still expected to change their names. A woman's name follows her husband's name on contracts. Perhaps you haven't noticed, but the name of the woman is often dropped in address form. The addressees are Mr. and Mrs. Kevin Duschaney.

Not long ago, married women couldn't get credit cards in their own names. These things were customary because of women's second-class status, and some are still practiced today. It should be no mystery to anyone that household chores and sex are areas of contention for married couples. Since cooking, cleaning and sex were all duties women were forced to perform while they were in subordinate roles, isn't it only logical to think that these activities would occasionally or regularly trigger anger in women?

But, don't you think women are overly sensitive about some things? Sometimes women just assume that men are chauvinistic assholes. They seem to want men to screw up so they can attack them.

You're right. Sometimes women *do* want men to make a mistake. At times they even dare men to say something wrong. Unfortunately, some women vent their anger in this way. Thousands of years of pain and anger have been passed on from one generation of women to the next, and some women release that anger through hyper-vigilance. Some women look for discrimination. It gives them an opportunity to exert their power and release their anger. But unfortunately, anger has momentum. Women have been mad for so long and for so many different reasons that it may take considerable time to heal all of their anger and resentment.

It's similar to the way women react once they finally decide to stop doing everything around the house. Some women complain for years about their husband's lack of help. Sometimes the anger continues even after the husband starts doing the chores.

That's because they think men should have been doing the chores all along. Women resent having to ask for a man's help. They think he should help without being asked. They seem to forget that when they were trying to coerce men into marrying them, they claimed that waiting on their prospective husband made them happy. It wouldn't take so long for men to pitch in and help around the house if women started out expecting collaboration. I don't care if my wife cooks for me or cleans the house. I just want to spend time with her.

It seems many men feel the same way.

Do women ever stop being angry? Once men start doing everything women want them to do, can they let it go?

Yes, but some women may not think it's enough for their husbands to start helping with the chores. Some women may not be happy unless their husbands are struggling and are angry about helping with the chores.

So, they want their husbands to see how miserable their lives were because of all of the work they had to do.

Right, if men aren't miserable doing the work, women feel as though *they* had no reason to be miserable.

But even if men anguish over the work, women still get angry. Men can't win. They're damned if they do and damned if they don't.

I know, in some cases they are. One day when one of my friends was complaining about her husband, I asked her, "Would you like to be married to you?" She looked surprised and after several seconds said, "No, I wouldn't."

I didn't have to ask her why, because I already knew the answer. My friend, just like many other women, wouldn't put up with the things that her husband puts up with. Anger is a big problem for many women, and it doesn't matter how men treat them or what men do for them, they're still going to be angry.

Remember the passage I read to you from *Divorced Dads* about how divorced men tend to recover from their anger sooner than women do?

Even though men usually get screwed in the divorce.

Good, you do remember. Women may stay angry for several reasons. One is to protect themselves from future pain. Another, whether justified or not, is to punish their husbands. Unfortunately, many men are willing to accept a woman's anger indefinitely, either because they are afraid of losing their wife, or they feel guilty for how they treated her, or both. Due to fear and guilt, a man will often take total blame for the marriage not working out. His willingness to accept full responsibility alleviates the need for his wife to take any responsibility for the failure of the marriage.

Some women also use anger to manipulate men. It's the whoever-gets-the-angriest-wins game. Anger is a defense mechanism. People, just like animals, use displays of anger to ward off attacks. Women use anger to intimidate men.

The first time a woman gets really mad and lashes out at her husband, she's likely to find out something she didn't know before: her husband is afraid of her. Angry people not only spur those around them to walk on eggshells, they motivate them to do exactly what the angry person wants them to do. Some women stay angry long after divorcing their husbands because, as long as they're angry and their ex-husbands feel guilty, they've got power over them and can feel justified, regardless of the men's behavior.

Though it usually takes a long time, men do eventually stop feeling guilty. That can trigger a new wave of anger in women. When men finally move on, they no longer care that their ex-wives are angry. In fact, many rarely think about their ex-wives at all. This can be a deflating time for a woman, because the intensity and duration of her husband's grief may have caused her to start viewing herself as a pretty hot commodity. When the ex moves on, her self-image may change. She not only loses the power she once had over her ex-husband, she loses her imagined title of "most desirable." It can be devastating for a woman to realize that her husband's grief had nothing to do with her; it had to do with his dependency on her. Ironically, this may have been why she wanted out of the marriage in the first place.

What do you mean by that?

Some women think their husbands care less about them than they do about all the services they perform. They feel as though their husbands know them only in the role of wife—not as individuals.

But that's not the man's fault. Men can't get their wives *out* of the wife role, not even for a minute.

That's because women think they have too much to do. They don't have time to step out of the role.

Why do women make everything so important? They create their own problems. Women act as though an unmade bed is a tragedy. I know women who won't leave the house on the

weekend unless all the laundry is done and the floors are clean enough to eat off of—I mean, come on, who cares?

They do.

But why?

Working women can't accomplish all the things that were expected of women in the past, but they still feel pressured to meet that standard.

But it's pressure they put on themselves.

You're right. They do pressure themselves, but you've got to understand, it's because they're afraid. Men often share a similar fear. Many men today who have lost their role as sole provider feel an absence of purpose. As a culture, we've been conditioned to believe that the only way to ensure another person's love is to be needed by that person. The same is true for women. Many of those who profess an eagerness to give up their domestic role continue to perform traditional tasks for fear that without them they will no longer be needed and loved. It's a catch-22.

Many women resist the expectations associated with being a wife. Those expectations not only seem unfair to women, they are unachievable in many cases. Women want their husbands to help because they often can't do it all, but a part of them feels like getting everything done is their responsibility. When household tasks are neglected, they feel they aren't doing their job and their self-esteem suffers. This is one reason why so many women are unhappy. Sometimes married women think their only choices are do it all and be bitter, or refuse to do it all and feel like a failure. Since neither choice is acceptable, a lot of women see divorce as an answer to the conflict.

So, it's a lose-lose situation for men, because women are in conflict with themselves.

You're absolutely right. That's why some of the women I interviewed said that life was easier without their husbands—even if they'd had helpful husbands. They no longer felt responsible for taking care of their husbands.

Here's an example. Last week I had dinner with a close friend who just recently married. During dinner, her husband called and asked her if, on her way home, she planned to pick up something for him to eat. Prior to his phone call, my friend was relaxed and enjoying herself, but while she was talking to her husband she started to look stressed. I knew exactly what she was feeling and I remember thinking to myself, *I'm so glad I no longer spend the majority of my time worried about if and what another adult is going to eat.*

Before my friend got married, we went to dinner every Thursday. Last week was the first time we had seen each other in three months and 30 minutes into our evening she stopped enjoying herself because of what she *felt* was her wifely responsibility—to guess what your husband wanted to eat and then either make it or go pick it up.

Why didn't she just tell him no?

Because she didn't want to feel guilty. She thought that he shouldn't even have asked her, because she wouldn't have asked him if the situation were reversed.

But he didn't know that, because he's not a mind-reader like she is.

The funny thing is, if she had said no, her husband probably wouldn't have given it a second thought. This is a perfect example of how women vacillate between guilt and anger. They're angry because of the expectations that have been placed on them, yet they feel guilty if they don't do what they think is expected of them.

Again, the expectations that go along with being a wife cause numerous problems for women. Things that matter so much to women while they are married don't matter nearly as much after they divorce. Women don't even seem to be as meticulous about their homes after they divorce, which is another reason they feel as though their workloads decrease when their husbands move out. I've known women who made their husbands' lives a living hell because they always wanted their house to look perfect, but when those same women got divorced, having a perfect house lost its priority.

It sounds like women try to put on a show for their husbands.

All of the pressure women put on themselves today is due to real pressure that was put on them in the past. If a woman didn't perform her marital duties well, her survival was in jeopardy. Today's reality doesn't matter much. Women and men are programmed with beliefs that were needed to survive in the past.

All of these things combined are why some women are angry, and have a tendency to stay angry.

Don't you think that women have a natural tendency to hold on to anger? Men get riled, blow up and then they're done with it. Women get angry, pretend they're not, and then one day explode. And even after they explode they remain angry.

I used to think holding on to anger was an exclusively female trait, but it's not. Men do the same thing. The difference is, women have always had a laundry list of reasons to be angry, whereas men haven't. But there is one thing that can cause men to stay angry for the rest of their lives.

I don't have to ask what that is.

I've found that men hold on to their anger over their partner's infidelity in exactly the same way women hold on to their anger about everything. It's not uncommon for a man who stays with his unfaithful wife to regularly punish her by throwing the fact of her infidelity in her face.

One woman I interviewed had been living with her boyfriend for seven years, hoping he would marry her. Her boyfriend's reluctance wasn't due to her having cheated on him; it was due to his fear that she might. He developed this fear because she had sex with him on their first date and regularly reminded her of this perceived indication of promiscuity on her part. So you see, holding on to anger isn't a male or female trait, it's a human trait. We hold on to anger to justify our own behavior and to manipulate the behavior of others. Do you really think the guy I was just telling you about sincerely believed that his girlfriend would cheat on him? Or do you think he pretended to suspect her because he liked the special treatment it earned him? Women hold on to their anger for the same reason. Because it works.

I think things are going to get worse. I don't see things getting better anytime soon.

We're definitely in a transitional period. Some women will continue to be blaming, defensive and angry until they feel comfortable with themselves, without reservation or explanation. However, the process would accelerate if men didn't allow women to treat them so badly. Some men are becoming as desperate to have a woman as women used to be to have a man.

But women have men by the balls. We're the ones who lose everything. We lose our families and our money.

Men often do get the worst of it. Many of my beliefs have changed since doing my research. I view the problems between men and women from both sides now. It's impossible to be angry or cast blame when looking at both sides of the story.

Ultimately though, men are responsible for their lack of parental rights. When women wanted the right to vote, they demanded and fought for it. Men haven't yet decided whether they really want equal rights and responsibilities as parents.

Well that's where we're going to leave off because I have to go. Tracey will be upset if I'm late.

Boy, you didn't learn a damn thing today, did you?

January 28, 2004

My conversations with Kevin are starting to wear on me. Not only do I find myself filled with anger that I thought was long gone, I also find myself going back in time and reliving everything, only now I'm reliving it from both sides. When I see the pain in Kevin's eyes, I can't help but think about all the pain that I caused. Yet at the time I was completely oblivious to it. I only saw my side. I thought men had it made. It didn't occur to me that men have to contend with the same mind fuck in regard to their feelings as we do in regard to our sexuality. If they show their feelings, they are considered weak. If they try to hide or control them, they are insensitive bastards.

Chapter 8

Men Send Flowers, But Women Who Cheat Give Oral Sex

Let's get back to the stages that men go through. You never finished telling me about them. After a man starts having an affair, what happens then? Does he want his marriage to end at that point?

No, men usually place more importance on their attachment bonds than women do because they have fewer of them, which is the same reason women place more importance on their attractions.

Women have fewer of them because they're pickier than men.

Right, but what's funny is, even though males are less selective than females, females put much more effort into attracting males. Our beliefs actually defy nature. In other species the males are often the "pretty ones." Why? Because in reality females are the choosers. Males pursue and compete for females. Men have few problems finding beautiful females because females work so hard to make themselves attractive to males. It would make more sense for males, the less choosy of the sexes, to put extra effort into their appearance, but until recently they didn't. However, I think young men are starting to feel a similar pressure with regard to their appearance. I wouldn't be surprised if we started seeing an increase in eating disorders among males. Older men are also feeling added pressure to maintain a youthful and attractive appearance.

The media are showing us more images of men and women of about the same age, as well as women with considerably younger men. The prevailing belief seems to be that females prefer older, distinguished men; however, "older and distinguished" equate to power and money, both of which women are beginning to acquire on their own. It's becoming more difficult for older, less attractive males to be with young, attractive females, which used to be quite common. Teenage girls and twenty-something females may continue to find older males attractive, but "older" for a twenty-year-old can mean thirty. So chances are, the males they find attractive actually *are* attractive.

I think younger women are attracted to older men for reasons other than power or money. Older guys know more and treat women better.

Experience isn't the only thing that enables older men to please younger women. Natural changes that occur in men as they age also make them sexually compatible with younger women. Men become more affectionate and attentive with age. Attention, affection, sexual skill and a diminishing sex drive make older men a good match for younger women. Older men and younger women are not as orgasm-driven as are older women and younger men.[1]

In contrast, older men may be at a loss as to how to treat a woman their own age. When I talked to married men in their thirties and forties, I found that many had little to no sexual experience with women of the same generation, unless it was a one night stand or a brief affair when they were younger. Most didn't know what it was like to be with a woman in her sexual prime because their wives were in their mid-twenties when they married. By the time the wives entered their prime, they had lost interest in marital sex.

How important to a woman is a man's appearance? I didn't think looks mattered as much to women as it does to men. I thought that women were more auditory and men were more visual.

Yes, that's true. It was an evolutionary necessity. Nature graciously made it easier for females to tolerate being forced into sex with old, unattractive, males. Women are more likely than men to close their eyes during sex for the same reason.

You are so full of shit! That's not true.

It makes sense to me. But, seriously, it's foolish to think that looks aren't important to females. Just as with males, appearance is more important to some than it is to others. I wish I could tell you the number of times I've heard or read that women don't care about a man's looks, sexual ability or penis size. And it's usually a man who's saying it. These beliefs are just wishful thinking on the part of men. Females are very much attracted to beauty; they are also attracted to strength and penis size. Among early humans, male strength was important because it helped ensure food and protection. Over time, females continued to desire strength in a mate, but strength evolved to mean money, which represents power or, more specifically, food, clothing, home and car.

Until recently, when women were asked if penis size mattered, their answer was, "No." If asked about the importance of physical appearance, their answer was, "Not important." If asked how often they thought about having sex with another man, they said, "Never." Even when asked about the importance of money, their answer was, "It doesn't matter." Why? Because that's what men wanted to hear.

The word *more* contributes to the problems men and women have in understanding each other. Just a few minutes ago you speculated that men are more visual and women are more auditory. Whenever it has been determined that one sex is "more" of anything, we fail to remember that the other sex still has that trait, only to a lesser degree. Males are more visual than females, but that doesn't mean that females aren't visual. Males like more sexual variety than females, but that doesn't mean females don't like sexual variety. Males are more aggressive than females, but that doesn't mean females are not aggressive. Males are more hairy than females, but that doesn't mean females don't have hair.

That puts it into perspective. Speaking of "more," you said men become more affectionate as they get older. Does that

mean women become less affectionate? Is that one of the reasons that Tracey is being so cold?

I don't know if it's so much that women are less affectionate; however, they do seem to need more separateness. It's not uncommon to hear men say that their wives are cold. I'm reminded of how young females describe their boyfriends. Women, on the other hand, often say that their husbands are boring—like males in their teens and twenties describing their young girlfriends.

What purpose is served by men and women wanting different things at different times?

I don't know. Maybe it increases the chance of healthy offspring. Maybe it's to keep old eggs from hooking up with old sperm.

Let's get back to what we were talking about. When they started having affairs, the men you interviewed didn't want to leave their wives, right?

Right. The men were more likely to say they loved their wives more than their affair partners, while the women were more likely to say they loved their affair partners more than their husbands.

So, did the men end their affairs?

The men usually ended their affairs or emotional connections the minute their wives tagged them.

What do you mean, "when their wives tagged them?" Did the men end their affairs because they thought their wives wanted to reconcile?

Yes, the husbands ended their affairs because they thought their wives wanted to get back together, which is what their wives wanted them to think—temporarily. They didn't want their husbands to give up hope and move on. So they made a quick tag in order to regain control over them.

I think that at some point the women began to derive a sense of power over their husbands and didn't want to give that up.

It's no different from the sense of power that males have over females at certain times.

Initially, many of the women I interviewed were inhibited from divorcing by guilt. However, they continued to live "in limbo" because doing so provided them security and control in their marriage while at the same time they were getting sexual gratification from their lovers. The women started getting used to their new lives, which included freedom, independence and stabilizing devotion from their husbands. And when that was threatened, they usually tried to eliminate the threat by performing oral sex on their husbands.

What?

I know it sounds bizarre, but it's true. Many men told me that just when they finally started to accept that their marriages were over, their wives would initiate a sexual encounter. I'd never have known had I not interviewed men who were separated, or whose wives were pushing for separations.

You're not really serious, are you?

Yes, I'm very serious and it's almost like clockwork, too. The women seemed to know intuitively when their husbands had met someone or were thinking about moving on. Several estranged husbands and men who were still living with their wives, but were regularly threatened with separation or divorce, reported that their wives initiated oral sex with them out of the blue.

So men send flowers when they've cheated and women give head.

Following these incidents, the men usually assumed that their wives were back, and everything was going to be okay.

I assume it wasn't.

No, it wasn't. Something made the wives insecure, so they tagged their husbands to regain their sense of control. Whether they were still living with their wives or separated, I consistently heard men say that when they finally accepted their fate, their wives surprised them with oral sex. And several of those men claimed that their wives had never before, or rarely, performed oral sex on them, not even in the beginning of their relationships.

I guess that explains why Tracey gave me a blow job the night before my brother and I left to go out of town for a golf tournament. We'd been having sex about once a month for the preceding year. I was floored because Tracey doesn't normally give blow jobs and had been acting very cold. It seemed awfully strange.

When I got back from my trip, everything returned to the way it had been. I left thinking that things might start getting better and couldn't wait to get home. I tried to kiss her and she seemed uncomfortable. Then she started running around the house acting busy so she could avoid me. Everything went back to the way it was before.

Tracey didn't want you sleeping with another woman while you were out of town. Both men and women use this tactic when they're feeling insecure. I think that's one of the reasons men insist on trying to have sex with their wives when their wives start losing interest—out of insecurity. It's either a conscious or subconscious attempt to hold on to their mate.

The women I interviewed used this method very effectively to hold on to their husbands even after they had initiated a separation. The men had begun to view their wives as unattainable. The constant rejection made them angry, but it also fueled their desire and made them hang on each time their wives tagged them. The rejection from their wives had triggered *limerence* in the men. They were obsessing, fantasizing and longing for their wives, while their wives were obsessing, fantasizing and longing for their affair partners.

You know, when Tracey started trying to avoid sex with me, I asked her several times for an explanation. She wouldn't tell me anything. Then we reached the point where we didn't talk about it at all, because whenever I brought it up she got angry and upset. Occasionally, I still made an overture, but she responded the same way every time. I don't think women know what it's like to be constantly rejected; I don't think they realize how bad it feels. When guys are dating, they're always in a position to be rejected. Then when they get married, the

rejection continues. After awhile, you get so angry you just don't care anymore. You make a decision to get married and be faithful, but you end up with a life of celibacy, and without any type of affection either. You get to the point where you don't care about the sex, but you can't understand why she has to be so cold. Do you have any idea what it's like to put your arms around a woman and have her look at you like you're a pathetic idiot?

I remember giving my husband that look.

What does that look mean?

It means, "I don't feel the same way anymore, but I don't know how to tell you." Women are afraid to tell the truth, and men are afraid to hear the truth.

The world is a hell of a lot more screwed up than it used to be.

Sorry, I can't jump on that bandwagon with you. People used to own people. Child abuse was considered discipline in the past, and it used to be okay to beat and rape your wife. If you think the world is worse off because of infidelity, then it should make you feel better to know that infidelity is nothing new. However, the reaction of women to their own infidelity *is* new.

I think people do have more affairs than they used to, because there's more opportunity.

Today we're seeing more women leave their husbands because of an affair. Divorce wasn't a plausible option for the majority of women in the past. And from what I've read, women are starting to have affairs much earlier in their marriages than they used to. I agree with you about there being more opportunities for affairs today, but the key word in that sentence is *more*. Opportunities were always there, but in the past people were more likely to have affairs with neighbors, friends, or in-laws than with co-workers.

You think that was common, huh.

Yes and still is. I heard almost as many stories about affairs between women and the close friend of their husband than I did about work-related affairs. I was surprised at the number of men I talked to who had lost their best friend as well as their wife due to an affair.

I don't know what could be worse than finding out that your best friend was sleeping with your wife.

How about finding out that your dad is sleeping with your wife?

What?

Yep, one of the men I interviewed discovered that his father was having an affair with his wife. The affair started after the father moved in with them.

Did the guy catch them together? Is that how he found out?

No, one week after this man's divorce was final, his dad told him that he planned to marry the ex-wife.

Something you said is bugging me. You said that women are having affairs earlier in their marriages, which implies that it's common for women to have affairs later in their marriages. If it is so common, why didn't I know about it?

That's exactly how I reacted. But mothers don't tell their daughters about their affairs or their difficulties with fidelity, so this is something women have to deal with on their own. Before I went to see a psychologist in hopes of getting information about how I was feeling, I asked my mom if she had had similar feelings in her marriage. She just smiled and changed the subject.

She didn't say anything?

No, not a word. But when she smiled at me, she had that, "I know what you're talking about" look on her face.

I'm surprised you didn't press her on it.

I tried. We were in a restaurant having lunch, and I asked her about it twice. Both times she changed the subject. It was apparent she was not going to talk about it.

I got similar responses from some close women friends after I wrote the information booklet. I was at a social function with eight women whom I had known for most of my life. We were sitting in the kitchen and the women's husbands were in the living room. I gave one of the women the booklet to read. All of the women were eager to read it, but their responses blew me away. Each woman read it and then handed it off like a bomb to the woman seated next to her. Without saying one word or making a single comment, the women passed the booklet around the table as though any sounds or sudden movements would cause it to detonate. The women who hadn't read the information were looking for responses and asking questions, but each woman reacted in the same way. She avoided remarking about the material by immediately commenting on the food.

One woman's husband walked into the room and wanted to know what we were reading. The women who had already read the information ignored him and continued talking nervously about the food. The husband started to ask again, and one of the women interrupted him to request a recipe. At that point, all the women who had read the booklet started exchanging recipes. It was hysterical. You wouldn't have believed the tension in that room.

I saw a look of recognition in each woman's eyes as she read through the material, yet none said a word. An older woman whom I had tried to interview when I started the research (she wouldn't talk) later walked me to my car. She looked at me rather matter-of-factly and said, "I'm sure after all your research, you understand why I couldn't talk about it." That was all she said, and it was the only feedback I got from that group.

Our mating habits form definite patterns, but we don't talk about what those patterns are. If you take into consideration that we have a 50 percent divorce rate, and also take into account the statistics on infidelity, it's apparent that these behaviors are natural and also quite predictable. But unfortunately, even when people seek help from a professional, they're not likely to get accurate information.

When you go to see a doctor about a physical problem, you describe your symptoms and the doctor tells you if your experience is normal. It should be the same when someone goes to see a psychologist. Even though psychologists usually make people feel as though their situations are unique, people's stories are remarkably similar. Several women I spoke with had gone to see a psychologist about their affair. More often than not, the psychologist helped them to justify their affair.

I think some of the women would have made different choices had they been given basic information. Imagine if a woman were told on her first or second visit to a psychologist that sexual relationships have a natural ebb and flow and that becoming somewhat disinterested in her husband sexually is normal. What if the psychologist also told the woman that at her age experiencing heightened sexual desire for someone outside of her marriage was common, and that acting on those desires would cause changes in her brain chemistry similar to those produced by drugs. Suppose the psychologist also asked the woman if she was ovulating when she met her affair partner.

I didn't even think about that. A woman's sexual appetite increases at that time of the month, doesn't it?

I don't know if that's generally true, but it seems women have a greater appetite for "strange" during ovulation. In *Mean Genes*, the authors say, "...There are four days a month when husbands ought to be especially attentive to their wives...Here's why: women who cheat on a spouse are most likely to do so during the four days surrounding their ovulation—their days of highest fertility! ...Furthermore, women are significantly less likely to use contraception with their lovers than with their husbands."[2] And Dr. Crenshaw writes in her book, "...Abnormally high PEA levels appear more often in women than in men. They typically occur at or near ovulation. This would seem to indicate a role for PEA in our desire to mate and procreate."[3]

I wonder how many women have met their alleged soul mates while they were ovulating. A few years ago, I tried to see if any of the women I interviewed had met their lovers during mid-cycle. I only found one woman who tracked her period and knew the date on which she and her affair partner had met. She had regular periods and had met her lover on the 13th day of her cycle. There's no way to know whether this woman was ovulating at the time, but I found it rather interesting. If someone's done a study on this, I would love to see it. This is basic information that women should have about their natural sexual tendencies. I think it might influence their decisions as to whether or not to divorce.

Psychologists may not know about all this stuff.

That's true. A psychologist I interviewed who had been counseling for over 17 years told me that she was starting to think women experienced some sort of midlife crisis in their thirties.

After 17 years she was "starting to think," huh?

She also said that, judging from her experience, women today are more likely than men to have affairs. I asked her if she was aware of the hormonal changes that women begin to go through in their late twenties and early thirties and she said she was not. During our conversation I found out that she had had an affair in her thirties, which resulted in her leaving her husband.

So much for getting help from the professionals.

Mental health professionals can be hampered by the fact that during marriage counseling women often don't disclose their affairs. When a woman has already stated that she wants to separate or divorce, counseling is usually a waste of time. Interestingly, some of the women who were having affairs prodded their husbands to go to counseling with them, even though they had no intention of working on the marriage. There really wasn't much the husbands could do to make their wives happy. The women didn't want their marriages to get better because they didn't want their affairs to end. A happy marriage would have created a conflict of interest.

If the women were seeing other men, why did they want to go to marriage counseling in the first place?

It helped relieve some of their guilt and made them feel as though they had done everything they could to save their marriages.

Yeah, everything but stop sleeping with someone else! I can't believe women participate in counseling under the

pretense that they're trying to work on their marriages when a divorce is what they're planning.

I talked to a woman just last week who recently started marriage counseling. I asked her if she was seeing anyone and she said no. However, later in our conversation she admitted that there is a man at her job to whom she is attracted. She said her attraction to him has nothing to do with the problems in her marriage. I asked her when the problems in her marriage started and she said they had been going on for about a year. Much later in our conversation, I asked approximately when she had met the co-worker to whom she is attracted. She explained that he was transferred to her office about a year ago. She is saving money and preparing for the possibility that things might not work out with her husband.

So she isn't planning to work on her marriage at all.

No, she isn't, but she feels better about herself by pretending to try. This was pretty common among the women with whom I spoke. They went back to their husbands after a period of separation, or continued living with their husbands after stating that they wanted a divorce. Although the women led their husbands to believe that they had recommitted to the marriage, many of them were either saving money or had postponed leaving until they met someone else.

But, weren't the women having affairs? Why were they waiting to meet someone else?

In some cases the woman's attraction didn't progress to the point of an affair, or the affair had ended and she was using the possibility of finding someone new as a means of getting through the withdrawal. It's kind of like using nicotine gum to quit smoking. First you break your addiction to smoking cigarettes, and then you have to break your addiction to chewing the gum. After an affair, people have to get over their addiction to seeing and talking to the other person. Then they have to overcome their addiction to thinking and fantasizing about the other person. After the memories fade, they have to give up the fantasy of there being a "right person." That's where people can get into trouble. They don't want to let go of that fantasy.

Fantasizing about a future mate gives people a buzz. Believing that a "right" person is out there who will make us happy makes us a little high—puts a little pep in our step. Consequently, fantasizing about a future mate is something we spend considerable time doing prior to marriage or when we have an affair. Even being attracted to someone after we're married can bring back the fantasy.

If the women you interviewed wanted their marriages to end, why, when their husbands finally said to hell with it, were they reluctant to let them go?

Because by the time their husbands started showing signs of moving on, the women had gotten used to the idea that the decision was theirs to make. They didn't want to give up control. Remember, the men typically didn't know that their wives were having affairs. Some of the women were waiting to see if their affair would turn into a permanent relationship, or were looking for a new relationship. Others just wanted to play around for a while. Furthermore, I think some of the women knew that their affairs wouldn't be as exciting if they weren't married, so they were reluctant to give up marital security for what could turn out to be a fantasy. The woman who was attracted to her co-worker is a good example. She didn't want to leave her husband until she felt some certainty about her impending affair.

The women were using their spouses as anchors while they were out scouting and building new relationships. The acceptance of this behavior by their husbands created an inflated, false sense of power in the women. Some of the women were rather arrogant. They seemed to be using their husband's devotion as a means to attract a new mate. By describing how heartbroken their husbands were they made themselves more attractive to their lovers. Their husband's grief became an advertisement. And when the women in this situation felt threatened—in other words, when they suspected that their husbands were starting to move on—they reached out to their husbands emotionally and/or sexually. The women were still very jealous at this point, and if their husbands showed any interest in other women they would in effect "mark their territory." Unfortunately though, this jealousy encouraged their husbands to feel hopeful.

It sounds like the women didn't want to be with their husbands, but didn't want anyone else to be with them, either. That's basically the same thing that men do to women.

It's the exact same thing. We make it seem like men and women are so different from one another. We forget that there is such a thing as *human* behavior.

As with men's behavior, women's behavior can be good, bad, and everything in between. Women are just as capable as men of abusing power. Males may grow up feeling powerful and superior to females, using them to get what they want and then discarding them, but when women get what they want from men, they are equally inclined to discard men, because in today's world they can. Women are now free to express this human trait.

For a while, I think we will continue to see such role reversals in relationships. Females will focus less on pleasing males. Eventually men and women will abandon traditional gender roles and find new ways of relating to one another.

In other words, women will continue to act more and more like men.

We've assigned certain behaviors to each of the sexes. Perhaps they don't truly reflect the gender to which we've ascribed them.

Blanket differences regularly drawn between male and female behaviors are often greatly exaggerated. Many of the beliefs we have regarding the opposite sex result from cultural conditioning. Today, females are being conditioned to focus on what they want as opposed to what males want from them. As women continue to leave their marriages, and as young females show less interest in being married to begin with, men might be the ones who develop long-term *limerence*.

You're saying that men, instead of women, will desire marriage.

Yes, it's already happening. Remember, *limerence* is experienced in the absence of certainty about the future of a relationship. So if females shun commitment, then males will be more inclined to want commitment. The women I spoke with who were looking for casual, uncommitted sexual relationships were surprised at how difficult it was to find likeminded men.

Sounds like all a guy has to do to have sex is act like he doesn't want to.

Lack of sexual interest on the part of a male usually drives the female crazy. Because females believe that males *always* want to have sex and will have sex with anybody, a man's lack of interest injures their self-esteem. Females can become quite defensive and angry when males reject their sexual advances.

Is it really that easy to manipulate people?

What do you think? Consider the sales techniques you use at your job.

I guess women are going to treat men badly for a while. They want revenge. Women are trying to gain self-worth at the expense of men. They want their cake and they want to eat it, too.

I agree with you, in some cases they do. But it's natural for people to want it both ways. Keep in mind, men were the ones who demanded fidelity from women, yet they also wanted the freedom to screw around. If that isn't wanting to have your cake and eat it too, then I don't know what is.

So, its payback time.

I hate to say it, but I think a lot of women feel that way. And it doesn't help matters at all that society is not acknowledging the problem. Not only does it fuel women's anger to continuously see and hear only one side of the story in the media and elsewhere, it also diverts attention away from the real problem occurring in relationships. Today, men are being cheated on and dumped left and right and seldom, if ever, do we hear anything about that.

Even in relatively recent books the idea is still perpetuated that men have a natural aversion and women a natural penchant for marriage. Let me read to you a passage that I find rather amusing. In *It's a Guy Thing*, author David Deida writes, "A woman's primary fantasy is to share love in a committed relationship with a man of great intelligence, humor and integrity. So, in our culture, the institution of monogamous marriage actually supports most women in their primary sexual fantasy yet deprives most men of theirs. When a man marries, it is understood he is making a sacrifice that a woman is not making." The author goes on to say, "...for a woman, it's often the fulfillment of her heart. For a man, it's often the denial of his inherent desire for multiple partners."

The author formed these conclusions, he says, "...after years of counseling both men and women."[4]

I think it's difficult, if not impossible, for a male therapist to know what his female clients really want. Several of the women I interviewed admitted that they didn't tell their male therapist the truth about their affair. They were concerned about what their male therapist would think of them.

To say that marriage supports a woman's primary sexual fantasy is ridiculous. Unfortunately, prior to marriage many women share a belief that is similar to Deida's. They also mistakenly think that marriage will not require a sexual sacrifice on their part.

Concerning a man's primary sexual fantasy: the men I talked with seemed willing to forego multiple sex partners in order to keep their partners from sleeping with anyone else. The ultimate male fantasy—sleeping with whomever they desired—wasn't worth having if it meant that their mates had the freedom to do the same. In order for males to indulge in their ultimate fantasy, females have to be monogamous. Otherwise, instead of bedding multiple sex partners, males would focus all their time and energy on keeping their mates at home—just as females have historically done.

I have to agree with you. Given everything that's going on between me and Tracey, the *last* thing on my mind right now is having sex with someone else. You were probably right when you said that men have to be one-hundred percent secure in their primary relationship in order to think about sleeping with other women.

The same thing holds true for women; however, few women have the false sense of security about male fidelity that males have about female fidelity. Consequently, instead of indulging in their sexual fantasies, they spend their time and energy trying to keep their mates faithful.

I feel stupid. Some of the things you've told me seem so obvious.

Don't feel stupid. People are regularly inundated with information that reinforces false beliefs. Not too long ago I heard a comedian comment that monogamy and marriage were invented by women and the church as a way to address female insecurity.

Although what he said is certainly the prevailing belief, it is contradicted by the facts. Most societies developed as patriarchies. Therefore, we can assume that men created the institution of marriage. Belief in this particular myth is intended to ease men's innate insecurity, as well as to create insecurity in females.

When do you think people are going to start talking about what's really going on? Don't you think men should know before they get married that their wives will probably stop sleeping with them, start screwing around and then divorce them? For the last 20 or 30 years we've been raising boys to be more sensitive and respectful toward females. Meanwhile we're raising girls to be just the opposite.

Some information has started to come out. But the information can easily be discarded because it is so contrary to what people have been conditioned to believe. Our current beliefs block contradictory incoming data. I'll give you a perfect example: Matt Lauer interviewed Dr. Judith Lipton and her husband, David Barash, the authors of *The Myth of Monogamy*. During the interview, Lauer mentioned that 50 percent of men admit to having an affair, 30 percent of women. He asked if these were accurate figures. Dr. Lipton replied, "No." Then Dr. Lipton's husband, Mr. Barash, said, "Probably not. The numbers are very squishy because, first of all, there probably isn't anything in human life that people are more likely to lie about than their extramarital sex lives. Secondly, men seem to be inclined actually to exaggerate the numbers a little bit. ...And women tend probably to downplay the numbers so as...not to feel like sluts. So the reality is it's probably forty to forty-five percent for both."

Shortly thereafter, Dr. Lipton said, "…Monogamy has a lot to offer. …We've been married almost twenty-five years, we're monogamous, we like monogamy. Then, Lauer asked, "Definitely monogamous?" Dr. Lipton said, "Yeah, definitely monogamous." And Lauer responded, "Although he just said that men…tend to lie about this."

Do you see how the information was disregarded? Barash said that men lie by exaggerating the numbers and women lie by downplaying the numbers. Yet Lauer appeared to be questioning whether or not Mr. Barash could be believed in regard to his fidelity. With the information that Lauer had just been given, it would have been more appropriate for him to say that women tend to lie about this and question *her* fidelity.

Frankly, I think it will take considerable time and repeated exposure before people will absorb the information.

And in the meantime, men will remain naïvely ignorant.

Kevin, the next time we see each other, there's something I really want to talk to you about.

Can you tell me what it is?

I'd rather wait until we have time to discuss it thoroughly.

April 21, 2004

The next time I see Kevin I'm going to ask him why he hasn't done something about the situation. It doesn't make any sense—and not just because it's out of character for him. I understand that even strong, confident men can become frightened and respond passively when their wives start rebelling. But Kevin has information that the other men I interviewed didn't have, and yet still refuses to act.

I know Kevin. I'm sure that by now he's done enough investigating and observing to know whether or not Tracey is really having an affair. If he felt certain that she weren't, he wouldn't spend so much time talking about it. At some point he'd have said that Tracey isn't exhibiting any of the behaviors I told him to look for. How can I convince him that his marriage will most assuredly end if he keeps pretending that nothing is wrong and continues to grovel for her affection. Women have no respect for men who cower from them. In fact, women are actually quite cruel to men who do.

Chapter 9

Women and Guilt

What did you want to talk to me about?

I want to know why you're not doing anything about your marriage. It has been almost a year since you started asking questions and looking for answers, and I'm sure the problem started some time prior to that. I don't understand why you haven't confronted Tracey. Do you really think you need more information before you can begin to resolve this?

If I go to Tracey and tell her that I know what's going on, I'm afraid it might prompt her to leave. I don't want her to become angry because she feels as though I'm accusing her of something.

I understand your fear. Most of the men I talked to were afraid of the same thing. They thought if they acknowledged the problem it would cause an abrupt demise of their marriage. They sensed that their wives were looking for a reason to leave, so they tried as hard as they could not to give them one.

Yes, that's it exactly.

Kevin, I've seen it happen over and over, and the statistics speak for themselves. You need to talk to Tracey and quit pretending nothing's wrong.

I know you think I'm weak for not doing anything, but I don't think you understand. If I have to swallow my pride

and play the fool in order to come home one more night, or wake up one more morning in the same house with my kids, that's what I'll do. Tracey can continue to make up excuses for why she needs to go out at night and she can sleep with whomever she wants, I don't care anymore. The only thing I care about is my kids.

Did you find out for sure that Tracey is seeing someone?

Well of course she hasn't admitted to anything, but I found a greeting card in her car from some guy. It was pretty sexually explicit. When I showed Tracey the card, do you know what she had the nerve to say? She said, "That's an old card from a guy I went out with before you and I met." How could she expect me to believe that a brand new-looking card was actually old and had accidentally found its way to the seat of her car?

Did you let it go at that?

Listen, I'm not stupid. I've done a little research of my own. I've talked to a lawyer and the bottom line is, if Tracey really wants a separation she can see to it that I am the one who vacates the house. The lawyer said that if Tracey and I get into a battle over the house or custody, I should be prepared for anything—including a false accusation of child molestation.

As for my interest in continued discussions about this, it's because I want to be prepared for what happens next. Tracey has done everything that you said she would do. You were even right in predicting when I'd get blow jobs. At this point I wouldn't be surprised if I went home and found her in bed with somebody.

Do not be afraid that Tracey will accuse you of abusing her or the children. If she threatens something like that, tell her she'll have to prove it. Men don't usually fight back—they don't defend themselves. Women can often get what they want simply by using threats. I'm telling you, Kevin, Tracey can't treat you this way unless you allow her to. Why do you?

I already told you why. I make my decisions based on what I have to lose versus what I have to gain. And for me, in this particular situation, the loss is too great.

Does any of this have to do with money? Are you afraid of losing your money?

No! I could care less about the money. I can always make more money. I'm only worried about one thing and that's my kids.

I thought Tracey was talking about getting her own apartment. Why do you suspect she might ask you to move out? Has she mentioned something?

Because before long I think it will dawn on Tracey that she doesn't have to be the one to leave. She'll realize that she could be the proud owner of a half-million-dollar home that's paid for. Because of my income, Tracey's lifestyle will continue to be pretty damn good even without me. Working will still be optional for her.

Unfortunately, we don't pay attention to things that don't affect us. For instance, you don't notice how many red cars are on the road until you buy one. The same thing has happened to me with this situation. I realize now that I know several men who've been through this, yet I never gave it a thought. I assumed they had all been lousy husbands. Now I know differently. I loved Tracey and I was committed to making her happy. But ultimately that's the problem. Women believe that "someone" can make them happy. Men don't tend to be quite as delusional in that respect. Men, for the most part, know that being happy is no one's responsibility but their own.

I think you're right. But I think you fail to see that men are falling into the same trap that many women are climbing out of. They're beginning to believe that they are powerless. Women once believed that they were powerless and, as a result, allowed themselves to be abused. Men are doing the same thing today. They are settling for the roles of martyr and victim as opposed to demanding what they deserve, which is equal rights to their home and kids.

Today, some women are using men as nothing more than props in their "fairytale fantasy" believing that men are worthless and disposable. Men can either buy into that belief or they can reject it. Men could not have established control over women if women had not accepted that what men brought to the table was more important than what they brought to the table.

Because male-bashing has become the norm in our society, the belief that women are more important than men is taking hold in the minds of both sexes. Your allowing this situation with Tracey to continue is a manifestation of this erroneous belief. You are surrendering your power and as a result you are now living in limbo.

Tracey's ambivalence about the relationship has led *you* to become ambivalent. That's what living in limbo is: ambivalence in one partner that leads to ambivalence in the other, which leads to indifference in one partner and, eventually, both partners. When both become indifferent, there's really no chance of salvaging the relationship. Living in limbo becomes a habit. The longer couples are stuck there, the harder it is for them to get out. They get used to it. It becomes part of their identity.

Living like this is draining your energy. You are gradually losing your self-esteem, and it won't be long before the choice to rebuild your marriage will no longer be an option. Neither you nor Tracey will have the energy to do so.

Life for you and Tracey has become little more than an endless array of conflicting thoughts and images about future pain or happiness.

Unfortunately, thoughts alone never lead to resolution regardless of how much time you spend thinking and mentally rehearsing possible scenarios. You're not going to figure out a way to make all this go away, and Tracey is not going to wake up one day and know whether or not she wants to stay married or get divorced. Experiencing doubt or uncertainty is very different from being in limbo. Limbo occurs when we mistakenly believe that a single decision has the potential to determine the level of happiness we will experience for the rest of our lives.

Although every decision has the potential to change our lives, no single decision has the ability to ensure or destroy our happiness or the happiness of others.

Aren't you the one who always says that one decision will never make or break you? You have always been successful, and have helped and inspired others to be successful because you have never allowed your fears to take over.

If you allow your fears to take over now and continue on your current path, Tracey's frustration over not being able to make a decision will end your marriage, and your frustration over her indecision will erode your feelings for her. You can only change your situation by acknowledging the problem and bringing it out into the open.

Order comes from chaos. People whose lives are a mess are actually (and unknowingly) on the cusp of order. To achieve order they have to recognize the mess and create an even bigger mess so they can sort, prioritize and eliminate. Through this process, order unfolds naturally.

If your closet is a mess, you have to make an even bigger mess in order to clean things up. Once you drag everything out, you are able to see what you have, what you don't have and what you need to throw away. Unfortunately, most people would rather live in the mess than make the necessary bigger mess.

That's because most people are afraid of change.

You're right. But the only thing worse than change is no change. Ironically, it's the lack of change that causes people to feel as though they're suffocating in their marriages. Aren't you the one who used to say, "Life is change—death is no change?"

I believe I did say that.

Kevin, if you take just one piece of advice from our conversations I hope it's this: if Tracey doesn't open up to you, let her go—don't try to hang on. If you hang on despite her lack of commitment, whether she means to or not, she will emotionally destroy you. There's no predicting the intensity or duration of your pain. It really is ironic that one of the cruelest things women do to their husbands is done out of misguided kindness. Women often destroy their husband's feelings because they don't want to hurt their husband's feelings. You need to trust me on this. Don't hang on. Tracey will never be able to make a decision if you do.

But how do you just let go of seven years of marriage?

It's easier if you are clear about what you are feeling. There's a big difference between grief and fear, and people often confuse the two, so it's important that you make a clear distinction between these two feelings. Nothing creates more fear in people than anticipating pain—not even pain itself.

For example, if I told you today that I was moving across the country, you would probably feel sad. We've been friends for so long and see each other so regularly, you would undoubtedly feel a sense of loss about my leaving. But you wouldn't be scared.

Likewise, if Tracey told you she was seeing someone and wanted a divorce, you would not be as fearful as you are right now. You would be shocked and temporarily scared, but you would do whatever needed to be done while moving through the grieving process.

Grief is nothing to be afraid of. It's predictable and, like any other feeling, temporary. Grief rises, falls and dissipates. As long as people don't try to stop their feelings from welling up, the feelings will eventually subside. However, when the pain starts to rise, people often fight it with thoughts such as, "This can't happen," "I won't let this happen" and "What can I do to stop this from happening?" They cut off or push down the feeling, which traps the pain inside. Fully experiencing the pain is the only thing that will relieve the pain.

Then again, many people don't want their pain to go away because they fear that love for their partner will go with it.

You're right. I hate that my feelings for Tracey are changing.

I know you do. So perhaps it's time to try a different approach before it's too late. Maybe you should stop letting Tracey use you as a security blanket until she solidifies a new relationship. Frankly, it's not beneficial for either of you.

I can see how it won't be beneficial to me, but I don't see how it would have a negative effect on her at all.

The longer a man holds on, the more pain his wife feels when he finally moves on. The duration and intensity of the man's grief leads her to believe that he is incapable of severing the relationship. She concludes that he will never love anyone like he loves her and will always be there for her. Nothing could be further from the truth.

I met one woman whose husband swore to her that he would never let go. He said he would always love her and be there for her even though she was living with another man. Unfortunately, the woman believed him. After three years of being separated and living with her boyfriend, she completely fell apart when her husband asked for a divorce so he could marry another woman.

It's quite common for women not to grieve the loss of a husband until after he moves on. Several of the women I interviewed had similar experiences. Didn't you say that you didn't start grieving the loss of your first marriage until a couple of years after it ended? Isn't that because it took Jill a couple of years to move on?

That's true.

People feel secure and invulnerable when they mistakenly think someone will continue to love them without their having to love that person back.

It's usually more difficult for men than it is for women to get over the pain, but they do recover and they do move on. And, like women, once they're done they're done.

When a man realizes that his wife wants to end the relationship, a window of opportunity exists to develop the type of relationship that the woman claims to want. At no other time is a man more willing to open his heart to his wife. But that opportunity doesn't last forever; it lasts only as long as the husband is scared, hurting and confused. So, the real task for the man in this situation is to find out if his wife wants a deeper relationship, or if she wants a *new* relationship. From my research, it's the latter.

I should have insisted on an answer to that question a long time ago.

If Tracey told you the truth, would you forgive her?

Yes, I probably would. Men often say that they would never forgive their wives or girlfriends for cheating, but that's not necessarily true. I think men make a lot of threats to prevent women from cheating. Women do the same thing. The double standard just makes it more effective on women than on men.

If you're serious, if you really could forgive Tracey, then she needs to know that. Like many women, she probably fears that she will lose her power if she admits to having cheated. Women realize that men have placed them on a pedestal and consider them incorruptible. That pedestal affords a woman tremendous power in the relationship. The thought of losing all that power is terrifying.

This will be the hardest thing in the world for Tracey to admit. Even women in good marriages rationalize that their husbands caused the problem. Tracey's identity is tied to being faithful. The fear of losing identity evokes the same response in humans as does the fear of death.[1]

People lie and keep secrets because they fear the reaction they'll get by telling the truth. We have all been conditioned to believe that we will be rejected and abandoned for certain behaviors. We condemn people for lying, but sometimes not nearly as much as we condemn them for telling the truth.

If you honestly believe that you can forgive Tracey, then tell her that. That's how your conversation with her should start. Tell her that you know something is wrong and that, whatever it is, she can tell you. Let her know that nothing she has done or could do will cause you to stop loving her.

I'm not sure I can say that. It may not be entirely true.

Is your love for Tracey contingent upon her fidelity? If it is, how can you say that you really love her? Wouldn't it be more truthful to say, you love her if…?

Marital love is highly conditional, which makes marriage the most potentially deceitful relationship we can have. The second most deceitful is the parent-child relationship. Parents often threaten to withdraw their affection if the children don't meet certain expectations. Husbands and wives use similar threats.

You know from experience that having extramarital sex doesn't mean that you don't love your spouse. Pretending that it does is just another lie intended to prevent married couples from cheating.

We are biologically driven not only to mate, but to mate with different partners. Given the right circumstances, everyone is capable of doing what they're biologically driven to do. And because we've been taught that sex is shameful, particularly under certain circumstances, our desire for sex is intensified. That's why sex is an addiction or obsession for many people. Our beliefs can not only increase the desire of people to have sex outside of their marriages, they can also intensify the high people get from doing so.

What other animal on the planet is crippled by its sexual attractions and encounters? How many birds lie in their nests unable to function because they can't stop obsessing over the hottie they saw last week? Animals aren't consumed by their sexual encounters because they don't feel guilty about them.

Feelings are constantly moving and changing. They are spontaneous flutters. People should never feel guilty about them. Every flutter is natural and temporary, unless the feeling is judged to be wrong. That's when fixations develop.

What you're saying makes sense, but I think you're minimizing how it feels to be cheated on.

Have I minimized it, or have I simply refused to maximize it? Life doesn't always meet our expectations. So what?

What do you mean, "so what?" I might be losing my family!

I'm not going to let you make this worse than it is. If you and Tracey split up, your family won't be lost. Your children will always be your children. Don't minimize your role in their lives and don't allow anyone else to either.

I don't want to diminish your feelings in any way, but try to remember that you have many reasons to consider yourself blessed.

I've seen and experienced a lot of pain over the last ten years. Most of that pain was unnecessary.

You can choose to believe that what's happening to you is a terrible tragedy, or you can see it for what it is—an opportunity to grow and experience something even grander. And that's not just some happy horseshit I'm feeding you in order to make you feel better. It's the truth. If you don't believe me, why don't you call Jill and ask her if, in retrospect, she's glad you cheated on her and left her for another woman. I bet she'll say it's the best thing that ever happened to her!

You would win that bet. She's very happy right now.

And what about you? Do you wish you had stayed with Jill or are you glad that you met Tracey and had the girls?

This is a bad time to ask me, don't you think? I'm kidding, of course. Obviously I wish that I had done things differently, but, yes, I'm definitely pleased things turned out the way they did.

The worst thing you're dealing with is the possibility that your wife's vagina has come in contact with another man's penis.

It doesn't sound like a big deal when you say it like that, but it sure feels like one.

That's because instinctively you are driven to pass on your genes. In the past a man's only guarantee that he was fulfilling that purpose was the virtue of his mate. If you understand this primal insecurity, then you can let a great deal of it go, because there's no need for it today. If you can let go of your primal fear, then you can let go of your conditioned fears—the fears you were taught to have. Fortunately, that shouldn't be too difficult for you because you already know from experience that Tracey's having slept with someone else doesn't necessarily mean she no longer loves you or wants to be married to you. Quite frankly, Tracey's having sex with someone else may not have anything to do with you at all. She's a woman, and at times women are biologically driven to gather the seed of more than one male.

So when you talk with Tracey, don't be afraid to hear the truth. Try to be nonjudgmental. I believe it is one of the greatest gifts we can give another person.

Again, I don't want to minimize your feelings. In fact it breaks my heart to tell you to be strong because I know that you, like every other male, are always expected to be strong. Your feelings do matter, but right now Tracey is in no position to care about anyone's feelings but her own.

You have the ability to help Tracey. Even though you're becoming more confused every day, you're still not as confused as she is right now. You can either fall into the abyss with Tracey or you can help pull her out of it.

Chances are, when she's out of this hole, she will be able and willing to help you deal with the pain you've been through.

Bearing these things in mind, do you think you can tell Tracey that you know something is wrong and that, whatever it is, she can tell you? Can you tell her that nothing she has done or could do will stop your loving her?

Maybe.

That's all you need right now—a belief that you can love her unconditionally.

Before you talk to Tracey, I think you should understand what she is probably feeling. As you know, when a person has an affair, guilt causes them to withdraw from the person they've cheated on. Tracey is likely to feel that she no longer deserves your love. She may also believe that if you really knew her, you wouldn't love her anyway. Just being around you probably makes her feel guilty.

However, she probably expresses her guilt by acting hostile towards you. With her lover, on the other hand, she feels accepted because obviously her lover knows what she's doing and chooses to be with her anyway.

If you remember, women in Stage 3 wanted to start over with a clean slate. They didn't want to be reminded of the things they had done. Being with their husbands made them feel terrible about themselves. So, it is imperative for Tracey to understand that you are not afraid to hear the truth and that you will listen to her without becoming self-righteous or passing judgment.

For many women, it's the secret that ultimately destroys the marriage. Many women simply can't forgive themselves because they have been conditioned to believe that cheating is an unforgivable offense for them.

Women attribute profound meaning to their affairs, because otherwise they'd have to consider themselves bad. Many women go on a wild goose chase attempting to figure out how they could have done such a thing. They look for reasons and justification. That's why we need to stop shaming females in order to control their sexuality. Ultimately everybody suffers because of it.

Do you really think it's the guilt that causes women to leave their husbands?

I think it starts with guilt. If they stop the affair, they feel guilt, but if they continue the affair, they postpone the guilt while masking it with sexual highs. Eventually, many women (and men) leave their relationships to avoid the guilt of having cheated in the first place. They see their marriages as tarnished. If they stay with their spouse, they have to think of themselves as a cheater. They only lose that label by starting a new relationship.

Some people really torment themselves with what they did and what it means—instead of simply viewing their indiscretion as a bad choice.

Yet there is much more to it than that. Women's guilt is extremely complex. I didn't completely understand all the opposing feelings involved until after one of my married girlfriends became attracted to another man at her job. I used to think it was simply the act of cheating on their husbands that caused women to feel so guilty. However, now I know there's more; there's another reason women become so guilt-ridden. The duration and the intensity of the guilt experienced by the women I interviewed was usually contingent upon whether the men they cheated with were single or married.

After my girlfriend went out for a drink with the guy she had been flirting with at her job, I asked her a question and was quite taken aback by her answer. I asked her if she could see herself ever leaving her husband. She said she could definitely see herself leaving her husband, but she added, "I wouldn't want to catch him off-guard with it. I would want him to see it coming."

Three months prior to this guy being hired by her company, my friend appeared to be happy. She loved her husband and she loved being married, too. However, my friend already knew that she might possibly be willing to walk away from her husband for the excitement of being with a new man. She also knew that it would take some time for her to turn her previously good marriage into a bad one. Leaving suddenly would come as a total shock to her husband and would also reveal the real reason for her leaving. Her husband as well as all of her friends and family would know she was leaving her marriage for someone else.

Although most of the women I talked to said they experienced tremendous guilt after they cheated, I think that many were misinterpreting the source of their guilty feelings. I think some were also confusing feeling torn with feeling guilty. The women who cheated with married men usually continued their affair and stopped feeling guilty—guilty enough, anyway, to discontinue the affair. Extreme, long-term guilt, however, seemed to be the norm for women who were having affairs with single men.

So, it was only the women who felt they had to make a decision who expressed being consumed with guilt. These women didn't want to stop seeing their affair partners. However, they knew that eventually their single lovers would meet someone else. So in actuality it wasn't guilt as much as it was their fear of loss.

The women who cheated with married men stopped feeling guilty and decided they could have both the husband and the lover. I believe the women who cheated with single men stopped feeling guilty for having cheated too. Many of them used feeling guilty as justification to continue their affairs. They cheated, they were going to continue to cheat, but to make themselves feel better and look better in the eyes of their single lovers they needed to feel really bad about it.

The affairs between the women and their single lovers often consisted of sex and conversations about how guilty the women felt. Some women said they sensed their single partner's level of interest in them decreased when too much time went by without expressing their guilt or the problems they were having in their marriages. It seemed their expressions of guilt and problems eventually became more like lines they were using to keep their lovers hanging on. The women were playing a balancing act, similar to the balancing act men play with their wives and the women they're cheating with, but with one difference. When forced to choose, women seem more likely to choose their lover over their spouse.

This is why some of the women experienced extreme ongoing guilt. Their ongoing guilt wasn't due to their having cheated, or continuing to cheat, on their husbands. It was due to the women knowing that if they were forced to choose they would choose the men they were having affairs with over their husbands. This is obviously something that disturbs women.

When women in committed relationships become attracted to someone outside of their relationship they are forced to come face to face with their apparent *lack* of commitment.

No one would ever suspect that females have a tendency to be rather uncommitted to males. Females are often dedicated to their goal of getting a commitment, or to getting married. They also can be quite committed to their marriages and families, but that does not necessarily mean they are committed to the men they are trying to marry or eventually do marry.

Since women have been taught that they want commitment, they seem to assume that their reason for wanting it is that they are naturally loyal and committed themselves. But the suddenness with which women are able to transfer their loyalties from one man to another certainly indicates a lack of commitment on their part.

Most women are aware they have this tendency and they are often quite disturbed by it. I think it's one of the reasons women take such a long time to extricate themselves from their marriages. If women left their marriages at the same time they actually *decided* to leave their marriages they would not be able to deny this tendency in themselves. It would be too obvious to them as well as to everybody else.

So, has your friend left her husband yet?

No, but her husband is now aware that she's not happy and he is doing everything in his power to make her happy.

Which is a big waste of time.

My girlfriend's marriage is a classic example of how the problem begins and evolves in many relationships today. Women are leaving their husbands and having affairs in an attempt to balance the scales that were typically unbalanced from the very beginning of their relationships. Built into each and every one of us is an automatic scorekeeper that is constantly assessing all our encounters and interactions with others. The need for balance is rooted in our brain chemistry, so balance is a necessity in relationships. As long as men and women are unaware of this automatic process that is constantly taking place inside their brain, their relationships will continue to follow a very predictable pattern. Men who marry women who used giving-without-receiving as a means to get the men to commit can expect to be cheated on or divorced by those women. This is exactly what happened to my girlfriend and it is also what happened to many of the women I interviewed.

My girlfriend met a good looking, successful guy and she wanted to marry him. A lot of other women wanted to marry him too. She waited patiently, pretending for three years that she didn't have any needs and it paid off for her. She ended up getting "the guy." But here's where her plan failed. Soon after my friend got married she realized that although she had won the prize, the prize wasn't worth having. It wasn't that her husband wasn't a nice guy. He was a very nice guy, but he was a guy who believed that she just naturally wanted to please him and that she didn't really need or want a whole lot in return. Five years and one hot single guy later, my friend has lost interest in being in a relationship that isn't balanced.

But her relationship is only unbalanced because she hasn't told her husband exactly what it is she wants.

By the time a relationship hits this point, a woman usually has few if any feelings left for her partner. Her automatic scorekeeper has unequivocally and, usually, irreversibly decided that she is giving more than she is getting. Because we've been wired to withdraw from relationships that are not balanced, women's feelings for their partners begin to erode; it's not uncommon for women to eventually feel less for their husbands than they would for a stranger on the street. The very method females use to get commitment from males is what initially begins the imbalance, and the things women do in the beginning of their marriages in order to feel like good wives are what tip the scale.

I still don't understand. Why does the decision have to be irreversible?

Because men don't usually find out exactly what their wives needs are until their wives are 100 percent done with the relationship—meaning their wives have lost all f eeling. When women start being specific to men about their needs, it's usually only to let their husbands know all the many areas in which they have failed. In other words, their husbands have already been fired; their wives are just giving them the reasons for the termination.

Either because of an imbalance that existed from the beginning of the relationship, or because boredom set in after the woman accomplished her goal, the only thing needed to tip the scale for the woman is an attraction to a "new" man. Many men are unknowingly playing a game of Russian roulette in their relationships with women. They're just one mutual attraction away from being replaced.

If you want to know the truth, a lot of women find that marriage doesn't offer a payoff commensurate with giving up their freedom and making a promise of fidelity.

There's only one way to fix this problem. Women have to communicate what it is they specifically need and want from their husbands. However, women can't put mind-reading or being good guessers among the items on their wish list.

Unfortunately for women, being specific about their needs comes with the negative side effect of feeling like a fraud. Women are particularly reluctant to tell their husbands what they really need because they're afraid if they do they will expose how deceptive they were during the courtship phase of their relationship.

No wonder women think men are clueless. Men would never guess that so much is going on behind the scenes in their relationships. Men have no idea that women not only plot to get them, but they also plot to get rid of them.

Try to keep in mind, all of these problems stem from the male's innate insecurity about paternity. That's what led to the suppression and denial of the female sex drive. It's also what created the false belief in women that they need to be something other than what they really are in order for men to want to be with them.

When you pull back all the layers, I think the root of women's guilt lies in the fact that deep down they know that they are not really anything like who they were conditioned and pressured to be.

Then I guess it is the guilt that makes women leave their husbands.

Yes, guilt often does play a role; however, I don't want you to get the wrong impression. Women do leave their marriages for reasons other than guilt. Women often leave their marriages because of the disappointment they feel over their real life not being what they had envisioned it to be—the discrepancy between their fantasy and reality. And women also leave their marriages for the same reasons that men leave their marriages: they no longer have the feeling that there is something to look forward to, the feeling of happiness in the future.

From the beginning of our lives, we're conditioned to eagerly anticipate particular events in the future. We look forward to enrolling in school, to each new grade, to getting our driver's license, graduating, going to college, starting a career, and especially to falling in love, getting married, and having kids.

But then what? For a lot of us, that's the end of looking forward, because we haven't conceptualized much beyond marriage and kids. Consequently, we're particularly vulnerable to extramarital affairs at this time in our lives.

Some type of fear often precipitates an affair. It could be the fear of a boring future, with nothing to look forward to, or it could be the fear of getting older. Many women approaching thirty experience the same trepidation as men approaching forty. They imagine it's their last chance at youthful happiness.

Fear of getting older, fear of not getting our needs met, fear of never accomplishing our goals, fear of dying, or even the fear of our spouse dying—any one of a number of things can be the catalyst.

I talked to one woman who, several years after her divorce, was able to pinpoint the fear that precipitated her affair. Her husband was going to a business conference and, prior to his leaving, she had a frightening thought. What would she do if he left her or if something happened to him? While blocking the thought from consciousness, she immediately scheduled an evening with her girlfriends during which she met another man. Their affair eventually led to the demise of her marriage. It took her years to figure out that the fear of losing her husband led directly to her leaving him.

Many men and women believe that disconnecting will protect them from becoming too dependent on their spouse. They mistakenly believe that disengaging or keeping the other at arms length will prevent overdependency. However, it only makes the problem worse. Remaining in a marriage from which we've physically and mentally disengaged creates a "security blanket" relationship. The dependency in the relationship actually increases and the relationship becomes nothing more than an unfulfilling habit, impossible to break. I think this type of relationship is the norm in our culture.

Didn't it say in the information you sent me that the women who got divorced regretted it?

It wasn't uncommon for women who had left their husbands and were several years into their next marriage to have regrets. I could see that they felt a little foolish for expecting the initial attraction to last. They left their first marriage for that feeling. When it was gone, they realized they were living a similar life with a different body lying next to them. Back where they started, they were once again struggling with disillusionment.

Since women have some of the same desires as men, what can men do to prevent their wives' cheating in the first place?

Men always ask me that. There's nothing that males or females can do to guarantee that their mates will never have sex with someone else. Women have to choose to be faithful, just as men have to choose to be faithful. Remaining committed and faithful will require effort on the part of women. It won't be long before there's an end to the sexual double standard, which means females will no longer be able to rely on shame or the excitement that comes from the chase to keep them faithful.

However, I think it would be easier for females to be faithful if we stopped referring to them as naturally monogamous, because then they would know and could put forth the effort necessary to remain faithful. Eliminating this false belief would also give males a chance. Males would know going in that females are unwilling to stay in relationships that are not intellectually, emotionally and sexually satisfying.

Women should also be prepared for the changes that occur in their hormonal balance—specifically, the unmasking of their testosterone. From talking to women, I now realize that these changes are drastically minimized. All of the over-forty women I talked to vividly recalled the time in their lives when they started losing interest in marriage and wanted to start doing their own thing.

One woman told me she could hardly stand being around her teenage son's friends because she was so attracted to them. Several women said they could have had sex with anyone except their husbands. And although females are always depicted as nurturers and caregivers, they don't necessarily retain that quality as they age. Single, older women who had already been married once usually said they had no desire to take care of a man. Most had no interest in remarrying and some never wanted to live with a man again.

Men and women should be prepared to experience a kind of subtle gender crossover as they age.

That little bit of knowledge would sure put an end to the battle between the sexes, wouldn't it?

It probably would. However, without this knowledge, the odds appear to be pretty good that many women in their sexual prime will step outside of their marriage when they get that "something's missing" feeling.

Tracey may have felt very dependent on you in the early part of your marriage. The independence she feels right now is probably a welcome relief. Like most couples, you and Tracey have habituated certain ways of relating to each other. Those may no longer feel natural to Tracey. Women can have a very difficult time pretending to be selfless, submissive, and sexless, both in and out of bed, after these changes begin to occur—and especially after having had an affair. It will be impossible for Tracey to go back to being who she was, because that's not who she is anymore.

You and Tracey can have a mutually fulfilling relationship again. However, breaking the patterns of relating that the two of you have fallen into will be extremely difficult.

How long will it take for Tracey to get over this other guy?

It isn't going to be easy. The withdrawal is intense. Because "love" is the high of all highs, the withdrawal from it can be the low of all lows. Tracey will most likely become depressed and she may not even be able to get out of bed for a while. Tracey will have to grieve the ending of the other relationship.

The grieving process may include Tracey's feeling tremendous anger towards you. She may view you as the obstacle that prevented her from achieving happiness. For a long time, she may question her decision to stay with you and regularly feel that the decision was a mistake.

Some doctors recommend an antidepressant when an affair ends. One of the women I interviewed said that if she had anticipated the extreme pain involved in separating from her lover, she would never have divorced her husband. Six months after the divorce was final, the relationship with her lover ended and she started taking antidepressant medication. She said that within three weeks she felt like her old self again and couldn't believe what she had done to her life. All of her feelings for her husband returned and she had no feelings left for the man who caused their breakup.

Withdrawel is harder for some people than it is for others. The higher a person gets from PEA, the harder the crash. Just as some individuals are naturally more prone to alcoholism or substance abuse, some are more prone to love addictions. We typically view the married who don't screw around and remain faithful as having good morals; however, due to differences in brain chemistry, some people are by nature less likely to screw around. Think of it this way: cocaine is the drug of choice for some, heroin for others.

And some people like both.

To a certain degree all of us like both, which is why we're so prone to infidelity. We get the heroin feeling from our spouse and the cocaine feeling from our lover.

Your chances of things working out will be greatly increased if Tracey doesn't feel as though she has to hide her feelings from you. The withdrawal process will be harder and last longer if Tracey doesn't think she can talk to you about her feelings.

I have talked with several people who tried to get over their affairs without disclosing them to their partners. Most of those people relapsed at the one year mark. After their affair ended, they spent a lot of time fantasizing about their lover; their memories became sacred to them. They in effect continued the relationship in their head. Then somewhere around a year after the first affair ended, another affair typically started.

Most gave tremendous significance to the fact that they still had thoughts of their affair partner even though a year had passed. When the one year anniversary of any significant event rolls around, our brains are flooded with sensory memories. Everything from the smell in the air to the temperature outside, or even the season itself can bring back the memories in full force. So it is not uncommon to experience intense withdrawal symptoms all over again. This caused several of the people interviewed to reach out for a new lover. It can take a couple of years to get over an affair and get back to feeling normal again.

So, even if Tracey decides she wants to work this out, a year from now I might have to go through this all over again.

If the affair is out in the open and the two of you aren't afraid to talk about what happened, you really shouldn't be too concerned with the one year mark. However, if you try to avoid what's happened, your relationship will probably wind up falling apart—maybe not now, but at a later date.

In many of the cases I examined, the man's reaction played a huge role in determining the outcome.

Try to think back to what it was like when you were young and you tried to break up with a girl. If the girl hung on, it probably made you that much more determined to end the relationship. Most of us are repelled by the fear and dependency of another person. The stories I heard all embodied a common theme: the husbands became desperate and the women saw them as pathetic. I know it sounds terrible to say, but that was the word used by the majority of women I interviewed to describe their husbands—pathetic.

Many women even placed a degree of blame on their husband because of his reaction. They wanted their husband to give them an ultimatum—a kick in the ass, so to speak.

The women couldn't stop their affairs. They hoped that the fear of losing their husband would snap them back to normal. People need boundaries. The women wanted their husbands to stop allowing themselves to be abused. People who are experiencing emotional problems are like little walking tornadoes. If you let them, they'll destroy everything in their path. The best thing you can do for yourself and an emotionally unstable person is to stop allowing her or him to abuse you.

Did you interview anyone who made it through this?

Yes, I did. I interviewed two men who handled themselves much differently than most of the men I talked to over the years. The first man took the initiative and filed for divorce after his wife expressed on several occasions that she was unhappy and considering a separation. Before the divorce was final, his wife was trying to reconcile, but he chose not to because of her disinterest in working on the marriage prior to his filing for divorce.

The other man dealt similarly with the problem, but he had an advantage. He had experienced a similar situation with his first wife. In that instance he lived in limbo for two years, doing everything he could to hold on to his wife, but nothing worked. Six years later he married again. Three years into that relationship, the second wife began to express her unhappiness. Though doubtful that he could endure the trauma of a second divorce, he took control and prevented any period of limbo.

He saw the similarities between his first and second wife's behavior and figured out right away that his second wife was seeing someone. He told her if she stopped her affair he would be willing to work on the marriage; however, he would not accept anything less than her whole-hearted effort. He insisted that separation was not an option because he recognized that separation is just a prelude to a divorce. He wrote his wife a letter and listed the changes that would have to occur in order for him to stay in the marriage. He gave me a copy of it. I will read a portion of his letter to you.

"Complaining is no longer acceptable. If you want me to do (or not do) something, you must tell me what it is. I do not expect you to read my mind and I will no longer try to read yours. If you want to have a mature, committed relationship you can expect one-hundred percent effort on my part; however, I will not allow my spirit to deteriorate because of your indecision."

His letter was direct and he set clear boundaries. Because he had been through the process before, he understood what his wife was doing even better than she did.

Separations are like cancer to a marriage. At some point, a person may need to take some time away from his or her spouse for a period of renewed self-discovery, but there's a difference between taking a vacation from everyday life and separating from it.

When people take vacations they are intending to return to their everyday life. However, when people separate they are hoping that they will eventually *want* to return to their life. People separate to try out a different lifestyle or to get something out of their system. Several of the women I interviewed said, "I want to *want* to be married." These women didn't seem to understand that wanting to want something means that you *don't want it!* Not wanting to be married went against their self-image. However, for many, so did cheating and leaving their husband. Since both options created the same image problem, limbo developed. The women were stuck, and the only way out was to make the husband the culprit.

People are confused when they're living in limbo. And little information is available about separation and what it really represents. A separation is a slow dissolution of the relationship. Women repeatedly told me that they couldn't decide what to do, but they were doing something. They were letting their marriages die slowly while either looking for, or already involved in, new relationships.

Some people stay in limbo for years waiting for clarity. For some, clarity never comes, because what they are really trying to do is avoid pain. They are hoping that one day it won't hurt to leave their spouse, or that one day they'll no longer desire to be with someone else and will want to return to their spouse.

Right now, Tracey probably feels as though she can't make a decision. It's as though she has weights around her ankles holding her in place. But if you talk to her and she is able to tell you the truth, that feeling will start to go away. Affairs lose their intensity when they're exposed.

The secret holds the power. The secret creates the excitement as well as the guilt. The secret will keep her in the grip of the addiction.

The euphoria of an affair is contingent upon feeling bad or guilty. It's the swing from feeling bad to feeling good—two opposing feelings—that keeps people addicted.

Infidelity would not produce such highs in people if cheating were not deemed horrible behavior. The euphoria people experience in affairs is created by and contingent upon guilt.[2]

If you genuinely don't believe that Tracey is a bad person

for what she's doing—if you don't believe that her behavior defines her as a person and if you are sincerely able to forgive her, some of her guilt will be alleviated. This will help break the addiction.

Conversely, trying to please Tracey will only make the problem worse by increasing her guilt and feeding the addiction.

Generally speaking, women feel more guilt than men for cheating, so their risk of becoming addicted to affair sex in general, and to their affair partners in particular, is greater.

I really have been doing the opposite of what I should be doing. I've only made the problem worse.

Most men do. So do most women when the situation is reversed. It's not uncommon for people to sit idly by while their relationships slowly deteriorate. Right now Tracey is trying to avoid pain by not making a decision. If you allow the situation to continue, it will lead to greater pain for both of you.

What happened to the guy you were talking about earlier—the one who wrote the letter to his wife?

The wife moved out for about three weeks. During that time, he operated on the assumption that she wasn't coming back. He didn't talk to her at all during that time. Instead he started to grieve the relationship's end in preparation for moving on. In other words, he didn't allow himself to get pulled into the game. He wasn't angry or bitter, just aware.

His wife ended up coming back home, but he'd have been okay if she hadn't. He said something to me that I'll never forget: when his second wife told him she needed a separation so she could find herself, having been through it before allowed him to read between the lines. His wife wouldn't need an apartment to figure out whether she wanted to be a doctor or an accountant; she would only need an apartment to sleep with another man. He commented that women today are a little careless and reckless— like a teenager with a new driver's license.

At first I was a little offended by that remark. Later I grasped the truth in it. Some women aren't accustomed to the choices they have and may not know exactly what they want. People who don't know what they want can create a lot of pain for those around them. So, in this regard, I understood what he meant.

But, I don't want you to think if you handle your situation the same way that man handled his, everything will be all right. You and Tracey could still spit up. However, by refusing Tracey the option of having both you and an affair, you will increase the probability of her making a choice.

Do you think people will eventually stop getting married altogether? Is that where you think things are headed?

I think a lot of people have already decided not to marry. People are beginning to choose the way they want to live instead of following a prescribed map. Marriage used to be the assumed way of life. Prior to that it was the necessary way of life. Now choice has entered the equation. Some groups claim that we are losing our morals. I think a more accurate assessment is that the people in the past had no choice.

What do you think about open marriage? Do you think that's the way people ought to live?

What do you think about open marriage? Do you think it's right?

No. I don't think its right at all.

Then you shouldn't have an open marriage.

Short-term relationships and alternative lifestyles are becoming more commonplace. But living under the same roof and sharing domestic responsibilities isn't what relationships are all about. The interactions of many couples consist of nothing more than conversations about what to do and what to buy.

I learned something pretty important last year when my friend, Kara, came to town for her birthday. I was planning to prepare her favorite dinner and dessert, but she suggested we go out to dinner instead. She also rented a car so I wouldn't need to pick her up at the airport. At dinner I asked her why she preferred to spend her birthday at a restaurant instead of relaxing at home. She said, "We don't get to see each other often, and the last thing I want is for you to be working while we try to catch up. I don't want my visit to cause you any extra work or stress. That's why I rented a car." She added, "The nicest thing you can do for me on my birthday is to give me your undivided attention."

I'll never forget that conversation. And I'll never forget how frequently I failed to give that gift in my marriage. I was constantly doing something, and I thought all my "doing" is what made me a good wife.

I think I know what you mean. Tracey still does some of the same things for me that she used to do, but none of that stuff really matters to me. I prefer she not do anything for me. I'd rather she just "be there" when we're together instead of being preoccupied.

I think it's especially difficult for people to give their undivided attention in long term, day-to-day living situations with another person.

Do you think that people should just go from one relationship to another? If separating from a spouse is like going through heroin withdrawal, shouldn't that tell us something? Maybe it means that jumping from one relationship to another isn't right.

Calm down, Mr. Defensive. First of all, I'm not saying that an individual's romantic relationships should be short-term or long-term. That's a matter of personal preference. And secondly, most of the suffering that occurs at the end of a relationship isn't due to withdrawal, it's due to fear. Marriage is set up to help eliminate fears and promote feelings of security; however, it usually has the opposite effect.

Even though humans are social animals, we usually don't form intimate relationships with anyone other than our spouse and children. This not only creates unhealthy dependencies, it builds fear and desperation. Such negative feelings wouldn't predominate if people had numerous caring, loving relationships.

The goal of relationships should be mutual fulfillment, not duration. Otherwise our marital relationships will continue being reduced to little more than endurance tests. As it stands now, people feel proud of themselves when they can stick it out, regardless of how miserable they are.

Many of the women I interviewed said they couldn't divorce their husbands because they'd feel guilty. Why does leaving make people feel guilty? Why don't people feel guilty about demonstrating on a daily basis their reluctance to express love to their partners? When individuals can no longer love their partner in the way they *would like to love* or in the way their partner *would like to be loved*, the kindest, most generous thing to do is to allow their partner, as well as themselves, the opportunity to give and receive love again in the way that they choose.

What I'm trying to say is, if people didn't believe that their relationships were supposed to last forever, they wouldn't experience so much pain when those relationships don't last forever. Our thoughts create our feelings.

I don't know if I believe that.

Research has established that thoughts change brain chemistry. Cognitive therapy works by changing your thoughts in order to change the way you feel.[3]

I'll give you a perfect example. When you first begin to wake in the morning, you probably feel good. But then you remember what's going on with you and Tracey, and that thought sends a jolt—almost like an electrical charge—through your body, filling you with anxiety.

That *is* how I feel in the morning.

So, nothing is wrong until you remember that something is wrong. But the point is, only your thoughts have changed. Prior to Tracey's telling you that she's not happy, you lived each day without questioning the permanence of your marriage. Now that's all you think about; however, the possibility has always existed.

That's true. So, if it's my memory that causes so much pain, are you saying I should just forget that Tracey and I might be splitting up?

No, but you can change your thoughts about the two of you splitting up. Regardless of what happens between you and Tracey, it will be for the best.

But I don't know if that's true. If we split up, I don't know that it will be for the best.

I do. Everything always is.

I'm telling you the truth. Most of the pain I experienced during my separation as well as after my divorce was unnecessary. If you believe that splitting with Tracey is a terrible thing, that will be your experience. Eventually you'll move on, just as you did after your split from Jill. Imagine how much less we would suffer if we knew before and during our experiences what we know after our experiences. Everything is going to be okay, and it's all for the best.

Having these two beliefs or, rather, knowing these two truths, will change your life. If every occurrence is viewed as positive and for the best, which past experience tells us is the case, then we could live in a constant state of joy.

Hey, I'm usually a pretty positive person, but I think that kind of attitude is a little unrealistic.

Think in terms of brain chemistry. If during positive experiences pleasure-producing brain chemicals rise (the rate at which these chemicals are produced increases), and during painful, negative experiences the same chemicals fall (the rate at which these chemicals are produced decreases), by viewing all experiences as positive we could keep those chemicals elevated and maintain a state of joy. The joy would exist independent of anything happening externally or outside of our own thoughts. Initially, this would require a great deal of effort. We would have to control our thoughts. However, eventually, thinking this way would become habitual and require little effort.

I hate to say it but that does make sense.

Unlike you, I used to be a pretty negative person. I'd never even tried something like this if I didn't think there was some logic and science behind it.

Not long ago, I made a remark to a man that I was seeing. Jokingly, I told him that he was unemotional and like a robot. He responded to my remark with, "The good thing about robots is they can be programmed." I was impressed by how quickly he responded; however, shortly thereafter it occurred to me that I probably wasn't the first woman to have made such a comment to him. Many women would probably have been frustrated by the way that he responded to my remark. But the truth is, he got it. He knew that he was the computer—and the progammer.

If you and Tracey split up, you can take as long as you want to accept that it's for the best. You are the only one who can write that program. We have the ability to change or create our feelings with our thoughts and through our behavior. In this regard, it might also be wise for you to view your brain as a pharmacy and yourself as its pharmacist who has the ability to either dispense or extract your feel-good chemicals.

So in other words, if you believe that your marriage shouldn't end and yet it winds up ending anyway, you will remain in pain until you prove yourself wrong. This is how feelings naturally change over time through behavior. Initially you may try to fight feeling better in order to prove yourself right, but eventually your experience will prove that it wasn't such a horrible thing. At odd moments you will find that you are not in any pain. You will catch yourself enjoying life. And much to your surprise you will find yourself one day in a loving relationship with another woman. This process could take between two and four years. That's approximately how long it takes individuals to fully recover from relationships where couples have been together for two years or longer.[4] However, it wouldn't take nearly so long to heal if people would choose to harness their thoughts and utilize their ability to create their own feelings, although doing so would require giving up the false belief that there is such a thing as a "right" or "special" person.

I think that's a rather depressing notion for most people.

Oddly enough, many people find the opposite to be equally depressing—the notion that everybody can be right or special.

People resist the idea that everyone is special because viewing some as more special than others is what allows our love relationships to become striving games—another opportunity where we can win or lose—another way in which we can swing from high to low and back again.

Our love relationships will continue to be game-like until we have played the game so many times and with so many different partners that we are literally able to predict the outcome before the game is even played. The difficulty sustaining relationships that many of us are experiencing today is necessary for our growth. We're in the process of learning through experience that no one is more right or special than anyone else. We're learning that it doesn't matter who we're with, our feelings change and can often be fleeting unless we ourselves create them through our own thoughts and behaviors. In the near future we will know this on a very deep level and we will no longer use one another to manufacture our feelings.

What's happening in your relationship with Tracey is the same thing that is happening to countless others in their relationships, and although painful, it's exactly what needs to happen in order for us to evolve. In other words, what's happening is perfect. It will eventually turn out to be for the best—just as everything always does.

Notes

Chapter 1
1. Theresa Crenshaw, *The Alchemy of Love and Lust: How Our Sex Hormones Influence Our Relationships*. New York: Pocket Books, 1996, pages 22, 39, 40, 283, 284, 285.
2. Terry Burnham and Jay Phelan, *Mean Genes*. Perseus Publishing, 2000, pages 189-193.
3. Lionel Tiger, *The Decline Of Males*. New York: Golden Books, 1999, page 57.

   Helen E. Fisher, *Anatomy of Love: The Natural History Of Monogamy, Adultery, And Divorce*. New York: W. W. Norton & Company, Inc., page 33.
4. Terry Burnham and Jay Phelan, *Mean Genes*. Perseus Publishing, 2000, page 69.

Chapter 2
1. Terry Burnham and Jay Phelan, *Mean Genes*. Perseus Publishing 2000, pages 176-177.
2. Kathleen Deveny, "We're Not In The Mood," *Newsweek*, June 30, 2003.
3. "J," *The Sensuous Woman*. New York: Dell Publishing Company, 1969, pages 85, 86.
4. Helen E. Fisher, *Anatomy of Love: The Natural History Of Monogamy, Adultery, and Divorce*. New York: W. W. Norton & Company, Inc., page 150.
5. Sanford L. Braver with Diane O'Connell, *Divorced Dads: Shattering The Myths*. New York: Jeremy P. Tarcher/Putnam, 1998, pages 134-135.

Chapter 3
1. Michael R. Liebowitz, *The Chemistry of Love*. Little, Brown & Company, 1983, page 90.
2. Helen E. Fischer, *Anatomy of Love: The Natural History Of Monogamy, Adultery, and Divorce*. New York: W. W. Norton & Company, 2001, pages 153-154, 171.
3. Terry Burnham and Jay Phelan, *Mean Genes*. Perseus Publishing, 2000, page 179.
4. David P. Barash and Judith Eve Lipton, *The Myth Of Monogamy: Fidelity and Infidelity in Animals and People*. New York: W. H. Freeman and Company, 2001, page 161.

5. Theresa Crenshaw, *The Alchemy of Love and Lust: How Our Sex Hormones Influence Our Relationships.* New York: Pocket Books, 1996, page 96.
6. Dean Ornish, *Love and Survival.* New York: HarperCollins Publishers, 1998, page 139.

Chapter 4
1. Joan Borysenko, *A Woman's Book Of Life: The Biology, Psychology, and Spirituality of the Feminine Life Cycle.* New York: Riverhead Books, 1996, page 121.
2. Theresa Crenshaw, *The Alchemy of Love and Lust: How Our Sex Hormones Influence Our Relationships.* New York: Pocket Books, 1996, pages 4, 114.

Chapter 5
1. Harvey B. Milkman and Stanley G. Sunderwirth, *Craving for Ecstasy: How Our Passions Become Addictions and What We Can Do About Them.* San Francisco: Jossey-Bass Publishers, 1987, pages 49, 104.
2. Michael R. Liebowitz, *The Chemistry of Love.* Little, Brown & Company, 1983, pages 60-61.
3. Harvey B. Milkman and Stanley G. Sunderwirth, *Craving for Ecstasy: How Our Passions Become Addictions and What We Can Do About Them.* San Francisco: Jossey-Bass Publishers, 1987, page 45.

Chapter 7
1. Sanford L. Braver with Diane O'connell, *Divorced Dads: Shattering The Myths.* New York: Jeremy P. Tarcher/Putnam, 1998, page 122.

Chapter 8
1. Theresa Crenshaw, *The Alchemy of Love and Lust: How Our Sex Hormones Influence Our Relationships.* New York: Pocket Books, 1996, page 31.
2. Terry Burnham and Jay Phelan, *Mean Genes.* Perseus Publishing, 2000, pages 184-185.
3. Theresa Crenshaw, *The Alchemy of Love and Lust: How Our Sex Hormones Influence Our Relationships.* New York: Pocket Books, 1996, page 31.

Steven R. Quartz and Terrence J. Sejnowski, *Liars, Lovers, and Heroes: What the New Brain Science Reveals About How We Become Who We Are*. New York: William Morrow, 2002, page 59.
4. David Deida, *It's a Guy Thing: An Owners Manual for Women*. Health Communications, Inc., Deerfield Beach, 1997.

Chapter 9
1. Gavin De Becker, *The Gift Of Fear: Survival Signals That Protect Us From Violence*. Little, Brown & Company, 1997, page 282.
2. Harvey B. Milkman and Stanley G. Sunderwirth, *Craving for Ecstasy: How Our Passions Become Addictions and What We Can Do About Them*. San Francisco: Jossey-Bass Publishers, 1987, page 104.
3. David D. Burns, *Feeling Good: The New Mood Therapy*. New York: HarperCollins Publishers, 1980, introduction.
4. Robert S. Weiss, *Marital Separation*. Basic Books, Inc., 1975.

About the Author

Michelle Langley has been a professional public speaker specializing in career development for over 11 years. She is currently working on her next book.

Additional copies of *Women's Infidelity* may be ordered from www.womensinfidelity.com